Marketing

SECOND EDITION

James L. Burrow

THOMSON

SOUTH-WESTERN

Australia · Canada · Mexico · Singapore · Spain · United Kingdom · United States

THOMSON

™

SOUTH-WESTERN

Marketing, 2nd Edition

Activities and Study Guide

James L. Burrow

VP/Editorial Director:
Jack W. Calhoun

VP/Editor-in-Chief:
Karen Schmohe

Executive Editor:
Eve Lewis

Project Manager:
Enid Nagel

Production Manager:
Patricia Matthews Boies

Ancillary Coordinator:
Kelly Resch

VP/Director of Marketing:
Carol Volz

Senior Marketing Manager:
Nancy Long

Marketing Coordinator:
Angela A. Russo

Manufacturing Coordinator:
Kevin Kluck

Art Director:
Stacy Jenkins Shirley

Compositor:
Custom Editorial Productions Inc.

Editorial Assistant:
Linda Keith

Cover Photo Source:
© Getty Images

Printer:
Malloy
Ann Arbor, MI

For more information about our products, contact us at:

Thomson Higher Education
5191 Natorp Boulevard
Mason, Ohio 45040
USA

Asia (including India)
Thomson Learning
5 Shenton Way
#01-01 UIC Building
Singapore 068808

Australia/New Zealand
Thomson Learning Australia
102 Dodds Street
Southbank, Victoria 3006
Australia

Canada
Thomson Nelson
1120 Birchmount Road
Toronto, Ontario
M1K 5G4
Canada

Latin America
Thomson Learning
Seneca, 53
Colonia Polanco
11560 Mexico
D.F. Mexico

UK/Europe/Middle East/Africa
Thomson Learning
High Holborn House
50/51 Bedford Row
London WC1R 4LR
United Kingdom

Spain (including Portugal)
Thomson Paraninfo
Calle Magallanes, 25
28015 Madrid, Spain

CONTENTS

CHAPTER 1	*MARKETING TODAY*	*1*
LESSON 1.1	WHAT IS MARKETING?	1
LESSON 1.2	BUSINESSES NEED MARKETING	3
LESSON 1.3	UNDERSTANDING THE MARKETING CONCEPT	5
LESSON 1.4	MARKETING'S ROLE TODAY AND TOMORROW	7
CHAPTER 2	*MARKETING IMPACTS SOCIETY*	*9*
LESSON 2.1	THE IMPACT OF MARKETING	9
LESSON 2.2	CRITICISMS OF MARKETING	11
LESSON 2.3	INCREASING SOCIAL RESPONSIBILITY	13
CHAPTER 3	*MARKETING BEGINS WITH ECONOMICS*	*15*
LESSON 3.1	SCARCITY AND PRIVATE ENTERPRISE	15
LESSON 3.2	OBSERVING THE LAW OF SUPPLY AND DEMAND	17
LESSON 3.3	TYPES OF ECONOMIC COMPETITION	19
LESSON 3.4	ENHANCING ECONOMIC UTILITY	21
CHAPTER 4	*THE BASICS OF MARKETING*	*23*
LESSON 4.1	CHANGES IN TODAY'S MARKETING	23
LESSON 4.2	PLANNING A MARKETING STRATEGY	25
LESSON 4.3	DECIPHERING CONSUMERS AND COMPETITORS	27
LESSON 4.4	MARKETING'S ROLE IN VARIOUS BUSINESSES	29
CHAPTER 5	*USING MARKETING RESEARCH*	*31*
LESSON 5.1	UNDERSTANDING THE NEED FOR MARKET INFORMATION	31
LESSON 5.2	FINDING AND MANAGING MARKETING INFORMATION	33

LESSON 5.3	USING MARKETING RESEARCH	35
LESSON 5.4	COLLECTING PRIMARY DATA	37

CHAPTER 6	**MARKETING BEGINS WITH CUSTOMERS**	**39**
LESSON 6.1	UNDERSTANDING CONSUMER BEHAVIOR	39
LESSON 6.2	WHAT MOTIVATES BUYERS?	41
LESSON 6.3	TYPES OF DECISION-MAKING	43

CHAPTER 7	**COMPETITION IS EVERYWHERE**	**45**
LESSON 7.1	TARGETING MARKET SEGMENTS	45
LESSON 7.2	POSITIONING FOR COMPETITIVE ADVANTAGE	47
LESSON 7.3	COMPETING FOR MARKET SEGMENTS	49
LESSON 7.4	LEARNING ABOUT THE COMPETITION	51

CHAPTER 8	**MARKETING FOR E-COMMERCE**	**53**
LESSON 8.1	WHAT IS E-COMMERCE?	53
LESSON 8.2	THE GROWING IMPORTANCE OF E-COMMERCE	55
LESSON 8.3	IMPACT OF E-COMMERCE ON DISTRIBUTION CHANNELS	57
LESSON 8.4	ROLE OF PROMOTION FOR E-COMMERCE	59

CHAPTER 9	**THE MARKETING STRATEGY**	**61**
LESSON 9.1	DEVELOPING A MARKET STRATEGY	61
LESSON 9.2	ASSESSING MARKETING MIX ALTERNATIVES	63
LESSON 9.3	ANALYZING PRODUCT PURCHASE CLASSIFICATIONS	65
LESSON 9.4	PLANNING FOR MARKETING	67
LESSON 9.5	DEVELOPING A MARKETING PLAN	69

CHAPTER 10	**DEVELOP A NEW PRODUCT**	**71**
LESSON 10.1	WHAT IS A PRODUCT?	71
LESSON 10.2	COMPONENTS OF A NEW PRODUCT	73
LESSON 10.3	PRODUCT MARKET CLASSIFICATIONS	75
LESSON 10.4	DEVELOPING SUCCESSFUL NEW PRODUCTS	77
CHAPTER 11	**SERVICES NEED MARKETING**	**79**
LESSON 11.1	WHAT ARE SERVICES?	79
LESSON 11.2	CLASSIFYING TYPES AND EVALUATING QUALITY	81
LESSON 11.3	DEVELOPING A SERVICE MARKETING MIX	83
CHAPTER 12	**PRODUCTS FOR RESALE**	**85**
LESSON 12.1	BUSINESS-TO-BUSINESS EXCHANGE PROCESS	85
LESSON 12.2	MAKING PURCHASING DECISIONS IN BUSINESS	87
LESSON 12.3	BUSINESS PURCHASING PROCEDURES	89
LESSON 12.4	RETAIL PURCHASING	91
CHAPTER 13	**GET THE PRODUCT TO CUSTOMERS**	**93**
LESSON 13.1	MARKETING THROUGH DISTRIBUTION	93
LESSON 13.2	ASSEMBLING CHANNELS OF DISTRIBUTION	95
LESSON 13.3	WHOLESALING	97
LESSON 13.4	RETAILING	99
LESSON 13.5	PHYSICAL DISTRIBUTION KEEPS THINGS MOVING	101
CHAPTER 14	**DETERMINING THE BEST PRICE**	**103**
LESSON 14.1	THE ECONOMICS OF PRICE DECISIONS	103
LESSON 14.2	DEVELOPING PRICING PROCEDURES	105
LESSON 14.3	PRICING BASED ON MARKET CONDITIONS	107

CHAPTER 15 **PROMOTION MEANS EFFECTIVE COMMUNICATION** **109**

LESSON 15.1 PROMOTION AS A FORM OF COMMUNICATION 109

LESSON 15.2 TYPES OF PROMOTION 111

LESSON 15.3 MIXING THE PROMOTIONAL PLAN 113

CHAPTER 16 **BE CREATIVE WITH ADVERTISING** **115**

LESSON 16.1 WHAT IS ADVERTISING? 115

LESSON 16.2 DEVELOPING AN ADVERTISING PLAN 117

LESSON 16.3 PUTTING THE AD PLAN INTO ACTION 119

CHAPTER 17 **SELLING SATISFIES THE CUSTOMER** **121**

LESSON 17.1 THE VALUE OF SELLING 121

LESSON 17.2 PREPARING FOR EFFECTIVE SELLING 123

LESSON 17.3 THE SELLING PROCESS AND SALES SUPPORT 125

CHAPTER 18 **MOVING INTO A GLOBAL ECONOMY** **127**

LESSON 18.1 THE EXPANDING WORLD ECONOMY 127

LESSON 18.2 HOW BUSINESSES GET INVOLVED 129

LESSON 18.3 UNDERSTANDING INTERNATIONAL MARKETS 131

CHAPTER 19 **MANAGING RISKS** **133**

LESSON 19.1 ASSESSING BUSINESS RISKS 133

LESSON 19.2 IDENTIFYING MARKETING RISKS 135

LESSON 19.3 MANAGING MARKETING RISKS 137

CHAPTER 20	**MARKETING REQUIRES MONEY**	**139**
LESSON 20.1	**MARKETING AFFECTS BUSINESS FINANCES**	139
LESSON 20.2	**TOOLS FOR FINANCIAL PLANNING**	141
LESSON 20.3	**BUDGETING FOR MARKETING ACTIVITIES**	143
CHAPTER 21	**WHAT IS ENTREPRENEURSHIP?**	**145**
LESSON 21.1	**WHAT IS ENTREPRENEURSHIP?**	145
LESSON 21.2	**ENTREPRENEURS' CHARACTERISTICS**	147
LESSON 21.3	**BUSINESS OWNERSHIP OPPORTUNITIES**	149
LESSON 21.4	**LEGAL NEEDS FOR ENTREPRENEURS**	151
LESSON 21.5	**DEVELOPING A BUSINESS PLAN**	153
CHAPTER 22	**TAKE CONTROL WITH MANAGEMENT**	**155**
LESSON 22.1	**MANAGING WITH A PURPOSE**	155
LESSON 22.2	**MANAGING EFFECTIVELY WITH A PLAN**	157
LESSON 22.3	**MANAGING MARKETING ACTIVITIES**	159
CHAPTER 23	**CAREERS IN MARKETING**	**161**
LESSON 23.1	**BENEFITS OF A MARKETING CAREER**	161
LESSON 23.2	**JOB LEVELS IN MARKETING**	163
LESSON 23.3	**MARKETING EDUCATION AND CAREER PATHS**	165
LESSON 23.4	**BEGINNING CAREER PLANNING**	167

Contents

Lesson 1.1 What is Marketing?
LESSON QUIZ

Directions: For each of the following statements, if the statement is true, write a T on the answer line; if the statement is false, write an F on the answer line.

______ 1. You see examples of marketing every day.

______ 2. There is no difference between effective and ineffective marketing.

______ 3. Marketing skills help you make better purchasing decisions.

______ 4. Credit card companies are directly involved in marketing.

______ 5. Marketing activities can be categorized within eight functions.

______ 6. Non-profit businesses do not conduct marketing activities.

______ 7. Communicating the value of products to prospective customers is a marketing activity.

Directions: For each of the following items, decide which choice best completes the statement. Write the letter that identifies your choice on the answer line.

______ 8. Successful businesses develop an approach to marketing planning that responds to
A. new products.
B. trends in the industry.
C. the needs of customers.
D. every situation.

______ 9. By studying marketing, you will learn
A. how businesses use marketing to increase their effectiveness and profits.
B. how new businesses are established.
C. how products are manufactured.
D. why consumers need a specific product.

______10. Distribution includes
A. creating a budget for marketing activities.
B. developing new products.
C. advertising.
D. determining the best procedure to be used so prospective customers can locate a product.

______11. Marketing-information management includes
A. obtaining market information to improve decision making.
B. pricing.
C. promotion.
D. delivery methods.

______12. Population trends
A. will reduce the number of new products developed.
B. show that most of the population growth will occur in developed countries.
C. will cause people in different areas to have vastly different economic needs.
D. will make it easier to distribute food.

Activity 1 • Apply the Marketing Functions

Directions: Describe how the following enterprises would use each of the seven marketing functions.

	Bank	Musical Recording Artist	Antique Clock Store	Drunk Driving Campaign
Product/Service Management				
Distribution				
Selling				
Marketing-Information Management				
Financing				
Pricing				
Promotion				

©South-Western Publishing

Lesson 1.2 Businesses Need Marketing
LESSON QUIZ

Directions: For each of the following statements, if the statement is true, write a T on the answer line; if the statement is false, write an F on the answer line.

______ 1. All business activities contribute in specific ways to the success of the business.

______ 2. Marketing cannot be successful for a low-quality product.

______ 3. Specialization of labor made it impossible to produce large quantities of a product.

______ 4. Self-sufficient people bartered for goods they needed.

______ 5. Marketing has existed since businesses began exchanging goods.

______ 6. A money system was developed to assist with the exchange process.

______ 7. A business must grow to a minimum size before it needs to coordinate its business functions.

Directions: For each of the following items, decide which choice best completes the statement. Write the letter that identifies your choice on the answer line.

______ 8. Self-sufficient people have to overcome
    A. bartering.
    B. specialization of labor.
    C. poor weather.
    D. all of the above

______ 9. In order to barter, both parties
    A. must want what the other party has.
    B. must have money.
    C. must travel.
    D. none of these

______10. Merchandising is
    A. making merchandise.
    B. transporting merchandise.
    C. selling merchandise made by others.
    D. accumulating merchandise.

______11. Operations includes
    A. storing products.
    B. maintaining equipment.
    C. servicing customers.
    D. all of the above

Activity 1 • Bartering

Directions: In the small town of Woodville, people still barter to acquire goods they need. Use the information below to make trades that will satisfy the town's residents. Identify the trades that each individual must make to acquire the item they want. Enter the name of each person they must trade with in the boxes on the same level in the order in which the trades must occur.

	Makes	Wants
Sara	Bread	Cheese
Max	Meat	Bread
Lynne	Dye	Bread
Jason	Apples	Dye
Melanie	Bread	Meat
Thomas	Cheese	Apples

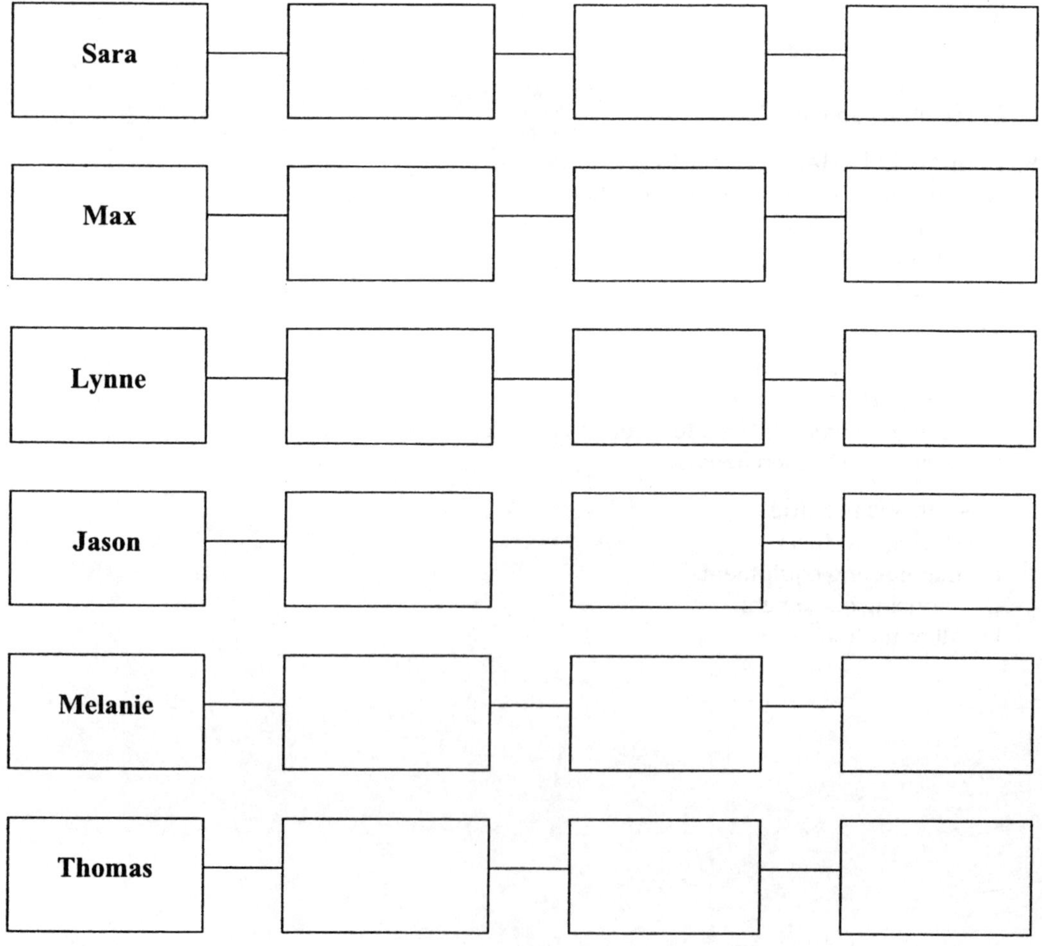

Lesson 1.3 Understanding the Marketing Concept
LESSON QUIZ

Directions: For each of the following statements, if the statement is true, write a T on the answer line; if the statement is false, write an F on the answer line.

_______ 1. Marketing was always an important part of business.

_______ 2. The most successful businesses are the ones that consider customers' needs as they produce and market their products and services.

_______ 3. A business must be able to identify what will satisfy customers' needs.

_______ 4. Some businesses rely on marketing activities to sell products after they are developed.

_______ 5. A marketing mix is the blending of three marketing elements—product, distribution, and promotion.

_______ 6. Companies that believe in the marketing concept operate differently than those who do not.

_______ 7. Price is the actual amount the manufacturer paid to make the product.

Directions: For each of the following items, decide which choice best completes the statement. Write the letter that identifies your choice on the answer line.

_______ 8. As consumers increased their standard of living and had more money to spend, the demand for newer and better products
A. increased.
B. decreased.
C. remained the same.
D. varied widely.

_______ 9. In the past, businesses could be successful by
A. producing more products.
B. increasing the amount of advertising.
C. increasing selling efforts for the products.
D. all of the above

_______10. Businesses that do not use the marketing concept
A. use extensive advertising.
B. sell more products.
C. develop products that customers need.
D. earn higher profits.

Activity 1 • Recycling Sells

Directions: As the marketing manager of a large manufacturing facility, you developed a marketing research program to determine consumers' responsiveness to using products identified as "manufactured with recycled materials." The results have indicated an 83 percent approval rating from consumers who purchase products that carry a recycling symbol on the package. Based on that result, you believe the company should consider using recycled materials.

Write a memo to the chief operating officer of the company explaining the study and its results. Encourage management to consider your recommendation and to use it as an important part of the marketing strategy. Be sure to indicate how this tactic can be used as a part of each marketing mix element—product, price, promotion, and distribution.

Activity 2 • Who's in the Market?

Directions: Develop a specific description of a potential market for the following businesses.

1. A health and fitness club

2. A cruise ship

3. A fast-copy printing business

4. A tax accountant

Lesson 1.4 Marketing's Role Today and Tomorrow
LESSON QUIZ

Directions: For each of the following statements, if the statement is true, write a T on the answer line; if the statement is false, write an F on the answer line.

______ 1. During the Production Era, production processes were very complex and many product choices were available.

______ 2. During the Sales Era, transportation systems were not well developed.

______ 3. Assembly lines were used during the Sales Era.

______ 4. There are some products that customers just won't buy.

______ 5. The role of marketing has remained the same for the last fifteen to twenty years.

______ 6. Marketing includes distribution, pricing, credit, and customer services.

______ 7. Marketing can help the business be more profitable by coordinating activities and controlling costs.

Directions: For each of the following items, decide which choice best completes the statement. Write the letter that identifies your choice on the answer line.

______ 8. Select the option that correctly identifies the development sequence of the philosophy of marketing.
   A. Production Era, Sales Era, Marketing Department Era, and Marketing Concept Era
   B. Marketing Department Era, Production Era, Sales Era, and Marketing Concept Era
   C. Production Era, Marketing Department Era, Sales Era, and Marketing Concept Era
   D. Sales Era, Production Era, Marketing Concept Era, and Marketing Department Era

______ 9. During the Marketing Department Era,
   A. customer needs became the focus.
   B. advertising was meant to convince customers.
   C. many new marketing activities were developed.
   D. all of the above

______10. Marketing managers
   A. are responsible for a large part of the company's budget.
   B. work with many people inside the company.
   C. work with many people outside the company.
   D. all of the above

Activity 1 • Competition in the Air

Directions: The airline industry in the United States has, in recent years, struggled to make a profit. Describe some of the ways various airlines have altered the elements of the marketing mix to try to remain competitive. Explain how the role of marketing has changed for the airline industry.

Activity 2 • Meeting Customer Needs

Directions: Select an item you own. Identify ten ways the product meets customer needs.

Lesson 2.1 The Impact of Marketing
LESSON QUIZ

Directions: For each of the following statements, if the statement is true, write a T on the answer line; if the statement is false, write an F on the answer line.

______ 1. Businesses that use the marketing concept do not benefit any more from marketing than any other company.

______ 2. Marketing helps a business satisfy customer wants and needs.

______ 3. Because marketing improves exchanges between businesses and consumers, individuals benefit from marketing.

______ 4. Understanding the marketing process and using the marketing concept will help you accomplish personal goals.

______ 5. Marketing identifies consumer needs that are not satisfied.

______ 6. When the marketing concept is used, the cost of production and selling prices increase.

______ 7. Countries that have well-developed marketing systems pay lower wages.

Directions: For each of the following items, decide which choice best completes the statement. Write the letter that identifies your choice on the answer line.

______ 8. Marketing includes
    A. transportation.
    B. promotion.
    C. financing.
    D. all of the above

______ 9. Marketing makes a company more likely to
    A. spend money.
    B. develop products.
    C. operate efficiently.
    D. all of the above

______10. Marketing skills help individuals to
    A. make dinner.
    B. exercise.
    C. find employment.
    D. follow instructions.

______11. To encourage international trade, marketing
    A. identifies shipping methods.
    B. pays lower wages.
    C. trains workers.
    D. all of the above

Activity 1 • Opportunities in the Marketing Field

Directions: Look in the employment section of your local newspaper. Identify three positions that require marketing skills. Describe the skills that are required and the responsibilities of the positions.

____

____

____

____

____

____

____

____

____

____

Activity 2 • Naming Rights

Directions: Identify the businesses that named the sports facilities in or near your city. Use the library or Internet to identify the amount of money paid by the businesses.

____

____

____

____

____

____

____

____

____

____

____

Lesson 2.2 Criticisms of Marketing
LESSON QUIZ

Directions: For each of the following statements, if the statement is true, write a T on the answer line; if the statement is false, write an F on the answer line.

_______ 1. Marketing always has positive results.

_______ 2. Many people believe that marketing causes unnecessary purchases.

_______ 3. The marketing activities of selling and promotion make up about 15 percent of a product's price.

_______ 4. Marketing can be used to misrepresent poor products.

_______ 5. Marketing has not made any impact on serious social issues.

_______ 6. Marketing can help prevent droughts.

_______ 7. One of the functions of marketing is to transport products to the location where they are needed.

Directions: For each of the following items, decide which choice best completes the statement. Write the letter that identifies your choice on the answer line.

_______ 8. Advertisements may be used to encourage consumers to buy
    A. a vehicle.
    B. a pickup truck.
    C. a pickup truck made by a specific manufacturer.
    D. all of the above

_______ 9. The long-term results of poor marketing can include
    A. a lost sale.
    B. a dissatisfied customer.
    C. A loyal customer.
    D. none of these

_______ 10. Marketing results in
    A. higher prices in the long run.
    B. no change to prices.
    C. lower sales volume.
    D. lower prices for consumers.

_______ 11. Social issues
    A. can be helped by marketing.
    B. are not appropriate topics for marketing.
    C. affect only a small part of the population.
    D. all of the above

Activity 1 • Social Issues

Directions: Identify an issue they can be affected by marketing. Design a poster that could be used in a campaign directed at the issue.

____

____

____

____

____

____

____

____

____

____

____

____

____

____

____

____

____

Activity 2 • Finding Data

Directions: The U.S. Census Bureau maintains demographic data, which they post on their Internet site at <u>www.census.gov</u>. Use the Internet or library to find answers to the following questions.

What is the population of your city?	
What is the population of your county?	
What is the average age of the population in your state?	
What percentage of the population in your state is male?	
What is the size of the average family in your state?	
What is the size of the average household in your state?	
What percentage of the population in your state graduated from high school?	
What percentage of the population in your state graduated from college?	
How many veterans live in your state?	
What is the second most common language spoken in your state?	
What is the largest industry in your county?	
What is the mean household income in your state?	

Lesson 2.3 Increasing Social Responsibility
LESSON QUIZ

Directions: For each of the following statements, if the statement is true, write a T on the answer line; if the statement is false, write an F on the answer line.

_______ 1. If consumers are dissatisfied with the actions or products of a business, they can organize a consumer boycott.

_______ 2. Social problems often lead to increased government regulation of business or increases in taxes to pay for programs designed to solve the problems.

_______ 3. The Better Business Bureau is a business protection organization sponsored by consumer organizations.

_______ 4. Consumer organizations encourage others to purchase products from boycotted companies.

_______ 5. Organizations and industries often develop a code of ethics to punish dishonest and improper conduct.

_______ 6. It is difficult to agree whether an activity is always ethical or unethical, but people place a high value on ethical business behavior.

_______ 7. Improper marketing can physically or financially harm customers.

Directions: For each of the following items, decide which choice best completes the statement. Write the letter that identifies your choice on the answer line.

_______ 8. Organized actions of groups of consumers seeking to increase their influence on business practices is
    A. consumerism.
    B. social responsibility.
    C. a consumer group.
    D. a social issue.

_______ 9. Consumer organizations
    A. purchase products.
    B. test products.
    C. sell products.
    D. all of the above

_______10. Whether an action is right or wrong should be determined based on
    A. political decisions.
    B. potential profit.
    C. the effects on the people directly involved.
    D. accountability.

Activity 1 • Loss Leaders

Directions: Many grocery stores and supermarkets use "loss leaders" to get consumers into their stores. Loss leaders are regularly purchased items that are sold well below their usual price (examples could include milk, lettuce, and bread). The business people using loss leaders believe that when people come to the store to buy the inexpensive item, they will buy many more items at regular or even higher prices. Consider the practice of using loss leaders. Then prepare two position statements using the following headings.

1. I believe the use of loss leaders is an appropriate business practice because. . .

2. I believe the use of loss leaders is a deceptive business practice because. . .

Lesson 3.1 Scarcity and Private Enterprise
LESSON QUIZ

Directions: For each of the following statements, if the statement is true, write a T on the answer line; if the statement is false, write an F on the answer line.

_______ 1. The marketing process is more scientific than creative.

_______ 2. There are enough resources available to meet everyone's wants and needs.

_______ 3. In a free economy, resources are free.

_______ 4. The United States has many of the characteristics of a private enterprise economy.

_______ 5. Consumers select products that they believe are able to provide the greatest satisfaction for the price.

_______ 6. The quantity of a product that producers are willing and able to provide at a specific price is demand.

_______ 7. In a private enterprise economy, the government uses laws and regulations to protect society from harmful decisions made by producers and consumers.

Directions: For each of the following items, decide which choice best completes the statement. Write the letter that identifies your choice on the answer line.

_______ 8. The basic economic problem is
   A. scarcity.
   B. monopolies.
   C. consumers.
   D. free economy.

_______ 9. Which needs are satisfied and how resources are distributed depends on
   A. scarcity.
   B. monopolies.
   C. consumers.
   D. the economic system.

______10. A decision to use resources in a way that results in the greatest profit for the producer is known as
   A. free enterprise.
   B. scarcity.
   C. profit motive.
   D. value.

______11. In a private enterprise economy, the success or failure of a business is determined by
   A. consumers.
   B. the government.
   C. the business.
   D. suppliers.

Activity 1 • Find the Resources

Directions: In the first column, find sources for the following raw materials or manufactured materials. If possible, identify a source close to your location. In the second column, identify a product that requires the resource when it is manufactured.

Source	Used In

Wood: _________________________________ _________________________________

_________________________________ _________________________________

Iron: _________________________________ _________________________________

_________________________________ _________________________________

Steel: _________________________________ _________________________________

_________________________________ _________________________________

Limestone: _________________________________ _________________________________

_________________________________ _________________________________

Corn: _________________________________ _________________________________

_________________________________ _________________________________

Wheat: _________________________________ _________________________________

_________________________________ _________________________________

Water: _________________________________ _________________________________

_________________________________ _________________________________

Glass: _________________________________ _________________________________

_________________________________ _________________________________

Cotton: _________________________________ _________________________________

_________________________________ _________________________________

Aluminum: _________________________________ _________________________________

_________________________________ _________________________________

Coal: _________________________________ _________________________________

_________________________________ _________________________________

Oil: _________________________________ _________________________________

_________________________________ _________________________________

 ©South-Western Publishing

Chapter 3

Lesson 3.2 Observing the Law of Supply and Demand
LESSON QUIZ

Directions: For each of the following statements, if the statement is true, write a T on the answer line; if the statement is false, write an F on the answer line.

______ 1. Understanding economics helps consumers and producers use their resources effectively.

______ 2. Macroeconomics studies how individuals make decisions about what to produce and what to consume.

______ 3. Consumers will pay more for a product if there is a large supply available.

______ 4. A demand curve demonstrates the relationship between price and the quantity demanded.

______ 5. Businesses use the resources available to develop products and services.

______ 6. As the price of a product increases, producers will manufacture more of the product.

______ 7. A supply curve and a demand curve should never intersect.

Directions: For each of the following items, decide which choice best completes the statement. Write the letter that identifies your choice on the answer line.

______ 8. The point where supply and demand for a product are equal is known as
    A. the demand curve.
    B. the market price.
    C. the supply curve.
    D. The points are never equal.

______ 9. Marketers are most interested in
    A. microeconomics.
    B. macroeconomics.
    C. individual product prices.
    D. supply.

______ 10. If there are no alternative products to satisfy consumers' needs,
    A. the supply will be large.
    B. the price will be low.
    C. supply and demand are unaffected.
    D. consumers will pay more.

______ 11. All of the consumers who will purchase a particular product or service comprise
    A. a supply.
    B. an economic market.
    C. an economy.
    D. a market group.

Activity 1 • Supply and Demand

Directions: Using the information from the following chart, construct a supply curve and a demand curve on the graph. Circle the point on the graph that identifies the market price. Estimate the market price and quantity.

PRICE	QUANTITY DEMANDED	QUANTITY SUPPLIED
$ 5.00	10,000	2,000
10.00	8,500	3,000
15.00	6,000	5,000
20.00	3,000	7,500
25.00	1,000	9,000

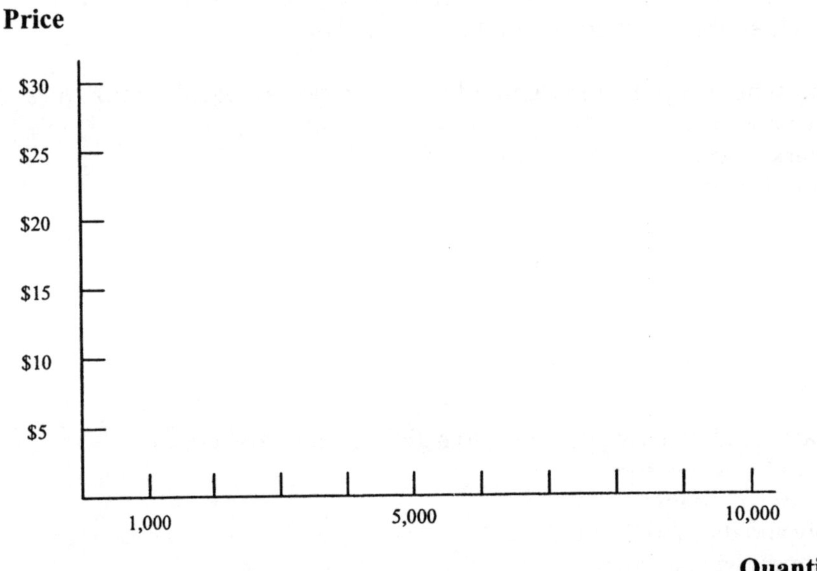

Estimate of market price $ _____
Estimate of market quantity _______

©South-Western Publishing

Lesson 3.3 Types of Economic Competition
LESSON QUIZ

Directions: For each of the following statements, if the statement is true, write a T on the answer line; if the statement is false, write an F on the answer line.

_______ 1. In pure competition there are a large number of suppliers offering very similar products.

_______ 2. A business in a purely competitive market has no control over price if it wants to sell its products.

_______ 3. In a monopoly, customers will pay a higher price because the supplier has no competition.

_______ 4. A utility company usually operates in a pure competition environment.

_______ 5. The airline industry is an example of an oligopoly.

_______ 6. By far, the most common type of economic competition facing most businesses is pure competition.

_______ 7. Elasticity of demand measures how much consumer demand for a product changes when the supply is increased or decreased.

Directions: For each of the following items, decide which choice best completes the statement. Write the letter that identifies your choice on the answer line.

_______ 8. A business without competitors operates in
    A. a pure competition market environment.
    B. an oligopoly market environment.
    C. a monopoly market environment.
    D. a monopolistic competition market environment.

_______ 9. Most retail businesses operate in
    A. a pure competition market environment.
    B. an oligopoly market environment.
    C. a monopoly market environment.
    D. a monopolistic competition market environment.

_______10. As a consumer, you will usually choose
    A. the least expensive option.
    B. the option providing the most satisfaction at the best value.
    C. the option that provides the highest quality.
    D. the most readily available option.

Activity 1 • Economic Competition

Directions: Companies will market products or services in quite different ways depending on the type of economic competition they face. A business in a monopoly will have a different marketing mix than one in pure competition. Select one of the following businesses: car rental business, airline, restaurant, construction company, gas station, supermarket, bank, or recording studio. Using the chart that follows, describe how each part of the marketing mix would be different for the four types of economic competition.

Business____

Marketing Mix	Type of Economic Competition			
	Monopoly	Pure Competition	Oligopoly	Monopolistic Competition
Product				
Price				
Distribution				
Promotion				

Name____ Date___________ Class ___________

Lesson 3.4 Enhancing Economic Utility
LESSON QUIZ

Directions: For each of the following statements, if the statement is true, write a T on the answer line; if the statement is false, write an F on the answer line.

______ 1. Form utility results from changes in the tangible parts of a product or service.

______ 2. A business schedules its hours to provide place utility.

______ 3. Automatic teller machines provide possession utility.

______ 4. Convenience stores that are open 24 hours a day usually provide time and place utility.

______ 5. Possession utility does not occur until the consumer owns the product.

______ 6. A video store provides possession utility.

______ 7. Economic utility supports the marketing concept.

Directions: For each of the following items, decide which choice best completes the statement. Write the letter that identifies your choice on the answer line.

______ 8. The amount of satisfaction a consumer receives from the consumption of a particular product or service is
   A. form utility.
   B. possession utility.
   C. time utility.
   D. economic utility.

______ 9. Packaging milk into smaller containers that can easily be handled by children is an example of
   A. form utility.
   B. possession utility.
   C. time utility.
   D. place utility.

______10. Lowering the price of a product provides
   A. form utility.
   B. possession utility.
   C. time utility.
   D. place utility.

Activity 1 • Communicating about Utility

Directions: Economic utility is an important concept for marketers because it describes how value can be added to a product or service to improve customer satisfaction. Businesses communicate the ways in which they are providing economic utility through advertisements and other forms of information. The headings on the items below describe each of the forms of economic utility. Review newspapers, magazines, and other sources of information about products and services. For each type of economic utility, identify one example of information describing a product or service feature related to that type of economic utility. Attach a copy of that information (or write the information if a copy is not available) in the appropriate space. Develop a brief statement describing why customer satisfaction should improve.

EXAMPLE OF FORM UTILITY

Reasons for improved customer satisfaction:

EXAMPLE OF TIME UTILITY

Reasons for improved customer satisfaction:

EXAMPLE OF PLACE UTILITY

Reasons for improved customer satisfaction:

EXAMPLE OF POSSESSION UTILITY

Reasons for improved customer satisfaction:

Lesson 4.1 Changes in Today's Marketing
LESSON QUIZ

Directions: For each of the following statements, if the statement is true, write a T on the answer line; if the statement is false, write an F on the answer line.

_______ 1. The earliest use of marketing was to move products from the producer to the consumer.

_______ 2. Marketing is more effective when it is not integrated into other business activities.

_______ 3. Marketing strategies are developed as a part of the business plans.

_______ 4. Marketing can help a business solve problems.

_______ 5. Many businesses reduce marketing efforts when faced with financial problems.

_______ 6. Spending money on marketing reduces a company's profit in the long run.

_______ 7. Businesses often fail because they don't understand and use the marketing concept.

Directions: For each of the following items, decide which choice best completes the statement. Write the letter that identifies your choice on the answer line.

_______ 8. The primary focus of the marketing concept is
   A. profit.
   B. efficiency.
   C. advertising.
   D. the needs of the customer.

_______ 9. To succeed, a business should
   A. know what customers will buy.
   B. study the market.
   C. use available marketing tools.
   D. all of the above

_______10. Today's marketers are continuously looking for
   A. problems.
   B. new products.
   C. new markets.
   D. value.

Activity 1 • Home on the Range

Directions: In America's past, horses, like marketing, served a different purpose. In the Wild West, horses were a means of transportation and a necessary part of a ranch's livestock. Compare how horses were marketed in the past with the way a dude ranch would market today.

PAST	PRESENT
Few Activities	**Variety of Activities**
Independent	**Integrated**
Problem-solver	**Opportunity-Provider**
Expense	**Investment**

Chapter 4

Lesson 4.2 Planning a Marketing Strategy
LESSON QUIZ

Directions: For each of the following statements, if the statement is true, write a T on the answer line; if the statement is false, write an F on the answer line.

______ 1. Without the marketing concept, a business will develop a product or service and then decide how to market the product.

______ 2. Various consumer groups may have different needs.

______ 3. Marketing and product planning should occur at the same time.

______ 4. Most of today's consumers are not well informed.

______ 5. Businesses that are not prepared for competition have a difficult time staying in the market.

______ 6. Some businesses do not see the specific needs of consumers as important.

______ 7. A business that believes in the marketing concept bases their business planning on increasing sales.

Directions: For each of the following items, decide which choice best completes the statement. Write the letter that identifies your choice on the answer line.

______ 8. If a company understands the marketing concept, its first step will be to
   A. identify the customer.
   B. develop a product.
   C. develop a marketing mix.
   D. distribute the product.

______ 9. Information collected by scanners at a grocery store is used to
   A. make change.
   B. adjust inventory records.
   C. describe available products.
   D. contact customers.

______10. Consumers with different needs require
   A. specialized products and services.
   B. more marketing.
   C. evaluation.
   D. market segments.

______11. Parts of the product decision that can improve customer satisfaction are
   A. research.
   B. customer identification.
   C. special features.
   D. promotion.

Activity 1 • Slogan Mix and Match

Directions: After a marketer has determined an appropriate segment for a product, the next step is to determine the marketing mix. One element of the mix is promotion. The goal of promotion is to direct a meaningful message to the target market about an attribute of the product or service. Some slogans become so well known that they live on after the product no longer exists or the business develops a new slogan. Place the letter identifying the company in front of the correct slogan. Based on your knowledge of the product and the slogan, identify the market segment that is being targeted.

Company	Slogan	Target Market
_______	1. You deserve a break today	
_______	2. Don't leave home without it	a. Coca-Cola
_______	3. Just do it	b. Microsoft
_______	4. Be all you can be	c. Toyota
		d. Nike
_______	5. Mmm mmm good	e. McDonald's
_______	6. I'd like to teach the world to sing	f. United
_______	7. Oh what a feeling	g. American Express
_______	8. I can't believe I ate the whole thing	h. U.S. Army
_______	9. Fly the friendly skies	i. Cambell's
		j. Alka-Seltzer
_______	10. Where do you want to go today?	

Activity 2 • Where You Belong

Directions: Describe the market segment that you identify with the most. Identify common characteristics and similarities.

____

____

____

____

____

____

 ©South-Western Publishing

Lesson 4.3 Deciphering Consumers and Competitors
LESSON QUIZ

Directions: For each of the following statements, if the statement is true, write a T on the answer line; if the statement is false, write an F on the answer line.

_______ 1. Most consumers are individuals who make decisions in a unique way.

_______ 2. A consumer may be aware of products but not make a purchase until a need exists.

_______ 3. A consumer evaluates the choices that are available after identifying possible solutions.

_______ 4. A decision can be evaluated by determining the satisfaction it delivered.

_______ 5. The most difficult type of competition businesses face is a market in which businesses compete with others offering very similar products.

_______ 6. Customers using the products and services of a monopoly business are usually satisfied.

_______ 7. Companies that use the marketing concept do not focus on specific groups of customers, but rather on all consumers in general.

Directions: For each of the following items, decide which choice best completes the statement. Write the letter that identifies your choice on the answer line.

_______ 8. When the same purchase decision is repeated again and again
   A. each decision is unique.
   B. the decision becomes routine.
   C. consumers fail to recognize the same situation.
   D. consumers follow all of the same steps to make the same decision.

_______ 9. The typical purchasing process begins when consumers
   A. determine the satisfaction the decision creates.
   B. identify possible solutions.
   C. recognize a need.
   D. evaluate options.

_______10. Consumers expect value from businesses in the form of
   A. higher quality.
   B. more service.
   C. lower prices.
   D. all of the above

Activity 1 • Decisions Decisions

Directions: A vacation is meant to be fun but it also means making plans. Planning a good vacation requires decisions. You can make decisions about your vacation before you leave home. Use the decision-making process to plan a vacation that doesn't cost more than $500.

Recognize a need.

____

____

____

____

Identify alternatives.

____

____

____

____

Evaluate choices.

____

____

____

____

Make a decision.

____

____

____

____

Determine satisfaction.

____

____

____

____

Lesson 4.4 Marketing's Role in Various Businesses
LESSON QUIZ

Directions: For each of the following statements, if the statement is true, write a T on the answer line; if the statement is false, write an F on the answer line.

_______ 1. A channel of distribution moves materials from consumers to manufacturers.

_______ 2. Product and distribution are important to producers and manufacturers.

_______ 3. When direct channels of distribution are used, producers and manufacturers rely on other businesses to deliver products.

_______ 4. Most service businesses do not use a channel of distribution.

_______ 5. Distribution planning is important because the service must be available where and when the customer wants it.

_______ 6. The gross profit margin is the amount a customer pays for a product.

_______ 7. Manufacturers are responsible for most final pricing decisions.

Directions: For each of the following items, decide which choice best completes the statement. Write the letter that identifies your choice on the answer line.

_______ 8. The difference between the price a business pays for a product and the price it sells it for is
   A. gross profit.
   B. net profit.
   C. markup.
   D. gross profit margin.

_______ 9. A middleman is responsible for adding
   A. product features.
   B. markup.
   C. functionality.
   D. the gross profit margin.

_______10. The price of a service is difficult to compare because
   A. a middleman is usually involved.
   B. different businesses may offer the service in a different way.
   C. the business has little control over the price.
   D. service businesses do not sell a wide variety of products.

Activity 1 • Ship It

Directions: Shelly plans to sell ceramic pottery she designs and makes. She doesn't think she can make or sell enough at this point to open a retail store. Instead, she will create an Internet site to sell her products. Before she starts, she must decide how to ship the products safely. Contact several shipping companies for information.

Alternative 1

____

____

____

Alternative 2

____

____

____

Alternative 3

____

____

____

Alternative 4

____

____

____

Activity 2 • College Degree

Directions: High school students get serious about choosing a college in their junior year. Colleges also choose students, accepting some applications and rejecting others. Colleges hope many students apply so they will have a larger pool of students applying for admission. Describe the marketing activities a nearby college has performed in the past year. Use the Internet, newspaper, and local library to collect information.

____

____

____

____

____

____

____

____

Lesson 5.1 Understanding the Need for Market Information
LESSON QUIZ

Directions: For each of the following statements, if the statement is true, write a T on the answer line; if the statement is false, write an F on the answer line.

______ 1. Most businesses try to satisfy the needs and wants of all possible consumers to attract more customers.

______ 2. An interactive kiosk is an inexpensive method of supplying information to customers.

______ 3. Customers' needs will remain the same over time.

______ 4. Consumers who have satisfied their needs can devote more resources to satisfying their wants.

______ 5. Effective marketing information improves decisions made by businesses.

______ 6. Effective marketing information does not affect the risk of making a business decision.

______ 7. Digital photography requires more cost and time than the production of traditional photographs.

Directions: For each of the following items, decide which choice best completes the statement. Write the letter that identifies your choice on the answer line.

______ 8. Businesses today compete by
    A. emphasizing location.
    B. emphasizing reputation.
    C. emphasizing price.
    D. emphasizing differences developed from product development.

______ 9. The marketing mix includes information such as
    A. consumer shopping behavior.
    B. product packaging.
    C. government regulations.
    D. all of the above

______10. To make effective marketing decisions, marketers need information about
    A. consumers.
    B. the business environment.
    C. the marketing mix.
    D. all of the above

Activity 1 • Cars, Cars, Cars!

Directions: Assume you are a car dealer who has been in business for five years. Since you have a dealership of mid- to high-priced new cars, you usually sell cars to buyers who are 25 years of age or older. Within the past year your inventory has expanded to include lower-priced new cars and used cars. As a result, you have discovered that a new market segment is coming into your dealership. This segment consists of 18–25 year olds who are purchasing their first car. You are interested in serving this segment but need to gather some additional information.

1. Are all 18–25 year olds in the same target market? Why or why not?

2. What information would be needed to qualify this segment as an effective market?

3. What important mix elements should be considered in attempting to reach this market?

Activity 2 • Around the World

Directions: Select a European country. Describe a target market that would be appropriate for a car dealer in the country.

Lesson 5.2 Finding and Managing Marketing Information
LESSON QUIZ

Directions: For each of the following statements, if the statement is true, write a T on the answer line; if the statement is false, write an F on the answer line.

_______ 1. Internal information is developed from researching factors outside the business organization.

_______ 2. A business must evaluate each source of information to determine if it meets the organization's needs in terms of accuracy, time, detail, and cost.

_______ 3. Marketing information can come from internal sources, external sources, and marketing research.

_______ 4. A customer club provides a business with information about its customers.

_______ 5. Businesses can't collect information that is more detailed than sales records.

_______ 6. Information about other businesses is available from internal information sources.

_______ 7. The most important performance measure for a business is comparing the current sales or costs against those of a previous month or year to determine if performance is improving.

Directions: For each of the following items, decide which choice best completes the statement. Write the letter that identifies your choice on the answer line.

_______ 8. An important source of information for marketers is
    A. an encyclopedia.
    B. a television show.
    C. customer records.
    D. all of the above

_______ 9. An external source of information for marketers is
    A. government records.
    B. sales records.
    C. income statements.
    D. all of the above

_______10. The five elements of an effective information system include
    A. advertisements.
    B. analysis.
    C. promotions.
    D. all of the above

Activity 1 • Information Scavenger Hunt

Directions: Use any available resources to answer the following questions.

1. What is the population of your community?

2. What is the average income of the residents in your community?

3. How many grocery stores are in your community?

4. How many brands of ice cream are sold at your local grocery store?

5. What is the name of the nearest minor league baseball team?

6. What is the population of your community?

7. Which states are touched by the Great Lakes?

8. How many tablespoons are in a ¼ cup?

9. In the year 2000, which state had the largest population?

10. Identify an event that happened on this date in history.

11. Where is Timbuktu located?

12. Who is at the top of the FBI's Top Ten Most Wanted Fugitives?

Lesson 5.3 Using Marketing Research
LESSON QUIZ

Directions: For each of the following statements, if the statement is true, write a T on the answer line; if the statement is false, write an F on the answer line.

______ 1. Marketing research is used when a business needs to solve a specific problem.

______ 2. To marketers, the United States and Europe have no substantial cultural differences.

______ 3. Numeric data is the easiest to organize for presentation and analysis.

______ 4. Customer responses to open-ended questions are not standard.

______ 5. Marketing research reports can only be presented in writing.

______ 6. A marketing research report should describe the purpose of the study and the research procedures followed to collect the information.

______ 7. Companies that have a production philosophy do not believe in marketing research.

Directions: For each of the following items, decide which choice best completes the statement. Write the letter that identifies your choice on the answer line.

______ 8. After reviewing the situation and the available information, a researcher
A. states the problem.
B. asks others to review the problem statement.
C. might be able to identify a solution.
D. all of the above

______ 9. Information already collected for another purpose
A. cannot be used for market research.
B. is not helpful for researchers.
C. is secondary data.
D. is primary data.

______10. A procedure in which everyone in the population has an equal chance of being selected in the sample is
A. a focus group.
B. random sampling.
C. marketing research.
D. all of the above

Activity 1 • Using Research to Make a Decision

Directions: Apply the principles of marketing research to the decision-making process in the following scenario. Describe how you would use this information to choose one of the jobs.

You are a senior in high school and need to save $3,000 for a car you have selected. You have two job offers and there could be additional alternatives.

Grocery store:

- Pay—$5.50/hour, weekend pay differential of $.25/hour
- Hours—15 hours per week; you must work either Saturday or Sunday; and you must close at least one night per week, which involves staying until 10:30 P.M.

Greeting card store:

- Pay—$5.00/hour
- Hours—18–25 hours per week, but you must work both Saturday and Sunday.

Define the problem.

____

____

____

Analyze the situation.

____

____

____

Develop a data-collection procedure.

____

____

____

Gather and study information.

____

____

____

Propose a solution.

____

____

____

　　　©South-Western Publishing　　　

Lesson 5.4 Collecting Primary Data
LESSON QUIZ

Directions: For each of the following statements, if the statement is true, write a T on the answer line; if the statement is false, write an F on the answer line.

______ 1. Open-ended questions are used while researchers are attempting to identify the problem for completing a situation analysis.

______ 2. Survey questions should encourage the respondent to answer with bias toward a specific answer.

______ 3. The respondents to a survey should be told that answers to a survey are confidential.

______ 4. Researchers can collect information by observing the behavior of a participant.

______ 5. Experiments occur when researchers happen to observe consumers' natural behavior.

______ 6. When marketers analyze research data, they will often calculate an average.

______ 7. Experiments are used more often in marketing research than surveys or observations.

Directions: For each of the following items, decide which choice best completes the statement. Write the letter that identifies your choice on the answer line.

______ 8. A planned set of questions to which individuals or groups of people respond is
   A. a survey.
   B. random sampling.
   C. a marketing research report.
   D. a focus group.

______ 9. A focus group is
   A. marketers who develop a survey.
   B. a small number of people who meet to discuss an issue.
   C. a list of specific questions to be included in a survey.
   D. none of the above

______10. Experiments operated in laboratories where researchers create the situation to be studied are known as
   A. focus groups.
   B. test markets.
   C. simulations.
   D. random sampling.

Activity 1 • Improving Airline Service

Directions: The airline industry is very competitive and lately has experienced a very small profit margin. A major U.S. carrier decided to survey its passengers to determine their opinion of the quality of the airline's service. Surveys were mailed to 7,500 passengers who had flown on at least two trips in the past six months. Responses to the survey are shown in the table. Calculate the percentages for each response to complete the table and answer the questions that follow it.

Questions	Responses					
	Yes	%	No	%	No Answer	%
1. Was your flight on time?	3,429		1,221		0	
2. Were you able to board promptly?	3,275		1,375		0	
3. Was your luggage check-in handled efficiently?	4,406		39		205	
4. Were the following amenities offered to you during your flight? Magazines Newspapers Pillow Headset	 4,013 1,984 2,543 4,439		 637 2,666 2,107 211		 0	
5. Were the beverages served promptly?	3,979		671		0	
6. Was the food appetizing and tasty?	3,261		889		500	
7. If applicable, did the airline personnel provide information regarding connecting flights?	2,341		267		2,042	
8. When given a choice of airlines, would you fly this airline again?	4,523		127		0	

1. What percentage of surveys was returned? Use a graph or chart to display your answer.

2. Visually illustrate the percentage results based on total respondents, by constructing a pie chart or bar graph for each question. Color code the responses to make the graphs more visually appealing.

3. What are the currents strengths, if any, of this airline's service?

____

____

4. What problem areas, if any, do you believe the airline should investigate further?

____

____

  Chapter 5

Lesson 6.1 Understanding Consumer Behavior
LESSON QUIZ

Directions: For each of the following statements, if the statement is true, write a T on the answer line; if the statement is false, write an F on the answer line.

______ 1. Successful businesses continually consider the customers' wants and needs.

______ 2. A final consumer buys goods and services to produce and market other goods and services or for resale.

______ 3. The hierarchy of needs was developed by Isaac Newton.

______ 4. Meeting your physiological needs is optional.

______ 5. A single product can fill more than one need.

______ 6. Consumers are at different levels on the hierarchy of needs.

______ 7. There are seven levels to the hierarchy of needs.

Directions: For each of the following items, decide which choice best completes the statement. Write the letter that identifies your choice on the answer line.

______ 8. The third level in the hierarchy of needs is
   A. security.
   B. esteem.
   C. social.
   D. physiological.

______ 9. Television broadcasters in a number of countries have few television commercials because
   A. they are subsidized by the government.
   B. companies will not pay for advertising.
   C. consumers do not respond to advertising.
   D. companies only advertise in America.

______10. Gaining respect and recognition from others satisfies
   A. security needs.
   B. esteem needs.
   C. self-actualization needs.
   D. all of the above

Activity 1 • Hierarchy of Needs

Directions: Place the listed items on the correct level of the hierarchy of needs, matching each item to the type of need it satisfies.

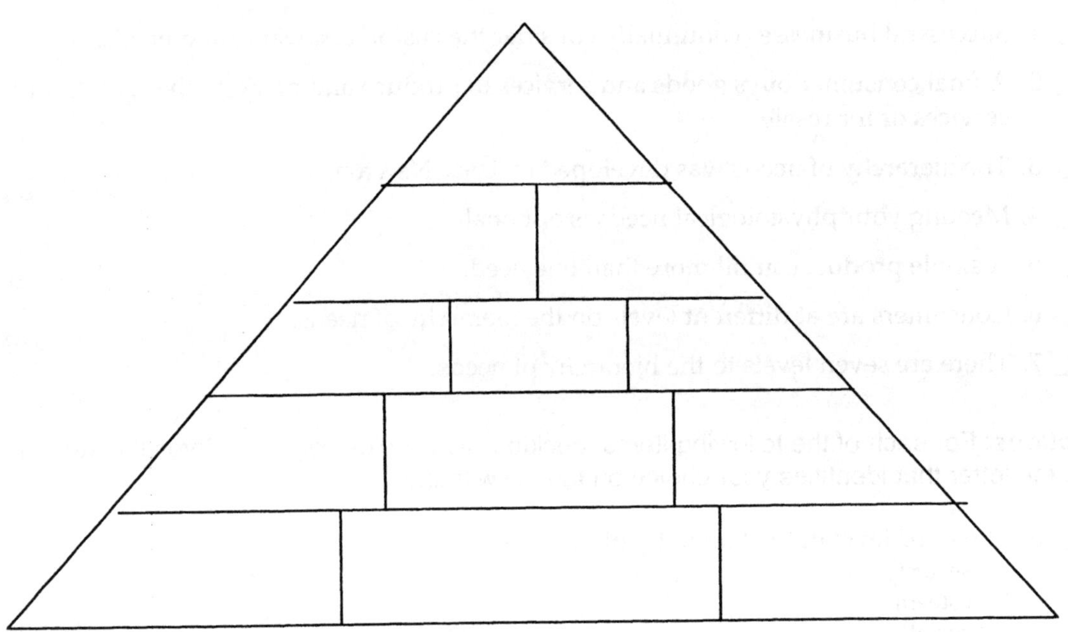

Buy a sports car.
Attend a wedding.
Take medicine for an illness.
Go dancing.

Join a baseball team.
Buy car insurance.
Write a novel.
Become physically fit.

Invest in a retirement plan.
Order a pizza.
Apply for a job.
Heat your house in the winter.

Activity 2 • Going, Going, Gone

Directions: Identify a consumer for the items listed below and determine if the consumer is a final consumer or business consumer.

Product	Consumer	Consumer Type
1. Diamond		
2. Nail polish		
3. Novel		
4. Potato		
5. Light bulb		
6. Computer		
7. Desk chair		

 ©South-Western Publishing

Lesson 6.2 What Motivates Buyers?
LESSON QUIZ

Directions: For each of the following statements, if the statement is true, write a T on the answer line; if the statement is false, write an F on the answer line.

______ 1. Advertisers can use fear to motivate customers to buy a product.

______ 2. Businesses have discovered that emotional motives are not very strong.

______ 3. Loyalty is a rational motive.

______ 4. Business people often base purchases on patronage motives.

______ 5. Consumers go through six steps when making a purchasing decision.

______ 6. The first step in making a decision is recognizing a need, desire, or problem.

______ 7. Consumers can find information in the phone book.

Directions: For each of the following items, decide which choice best completes the statement. Write the letter that identifies your choice on the answer line.

______ 8. If you shop in the same store your parents shopped, your motivation for choosing the same retailer is
    A. emotional.
    B. rational.
    C. patronage.
    D. all of the above

______ 9. Businesses want less competition so they encourage
    A. emotional motives.
    B. rational motives.
    C. patronage motives.
    D. all of the above

______ 10. Consumers evaluate their satisfaction with a product
    A. when they purchase the product.
    B. when they search for information.
    C. after the product has been purchased.
    D. when the need is recognized.

Activity 1 • Changing Cultures

Directions: Using your school or public library, investigate the changes in our culture that have occurred in the past 30 years. Most of the information will probably come from periodicals. Locate at least six cultural changes that have occurred and determine how marketers have responded to these changes with new or improved products or services. You may want to focus your study on a specific cultural group.

1. ____

   Response:____

   ____

   ____

2. ____

   Response:____

   ____

   ____

3. ____

   Response:____

   ____

   ____

4. ____

   Response:____

   ____

   ____

5. ____

   Response:____

   ____

   ____

6. ____

   Response:____

   ____

   ____

Lesson 6.3 Types of Decision-Making
LESSON QUIZ

Directions: For each of the following statements, if the statement is true, write a T on the answer line; if the statement is false, write an F on the answer line.

______ 1. The factors that influence a customer's buying decision are not important to marketers.

______ 2. External factors do not influence our purchase decisions.

______ 3. A company reaches the breakeven point when it buys more merchandise than it sells.

______ 4. Personality is a well-defined, enduring pattern of behavior.

______ 5. Your favorite color is influenced by your personality.

______ 6. Businesses use limited decision-making to select office furniture.

______ 7. Marketers try to encourage brand loyalty.

Directions: For each of the following items, decide which choice best completes the statement. Write the letter that identifies your choice on the answer line.

______ 8. A set of beliefs or attitudes that are passed on from generation to generation are
   A. personality characteristics.
   B. culture.
   C. social class.
   D. reference group.

______ 9. Your reference group determines
   A. the money you have available for purchases.
   B. your neighborhood.
   C. your values and attitudes.
   D. all of the above

______10. Direct mail is
   A. coupons.
   B. catalogs.
   C. promotional fliers.
   D. all of the above

Activity 1 • Promoting People

Directions: As the media specialist for a presidential candidate, your research indicates that this will be a very emotional election. Many people are out of work because of the poor economy. Based on this information and your knowledge of buying motives and the consumer decision-making process, how would you market your candidate? Include a discussion of buying motives and the decision-making process consumers use in determining how to vote.

Buying Motives: ____

____

Decision-making process:

Need Recognition: ____

____

Information Search:____

____

Alternative Evaluation:____

____

Purchase: ____

____

Postpurchase Evaluation: ____

____

Activity 2 • Determining the Types of Decisions

Directions: Classify the following products as either requiring routine, limited, or extensive decision-making and indicate a reason why you made the selection. You might decide that more than one type of decision-making is possible. If so, indicate all possibilities and give reasons for your answers.

1. **Light bulbs:**____

   Reason:____

   ____

2. **Financial planning services:**____

   Reason:____

   ____

3. **Personal computer :**____

   Reason:____

   ____

 ©South-Western Publishing

Lesson 7.1 Targeting Market Segments
LESSON QUIZ

Directions: For each of the following statements, if the statement is true, write a T on the answer line; if the statement is false, write an F on the answer line.

______ 1. The characteristics of a market segment result in similar product or service needs.

______ 2. You can belong to only one market segment.

______ 3. Companies vary in size and therefore the group of customers they want to reach also varies in size.

______ 4. The frequency with which consumers use a product can place them in a market segment targeted by the product manufacturer.

______ 5. Business markets are segmented in the same way that consumer markets are segmented.

______ 6. The market share is the total revenue that can be obtained from the market segment.

______ 7. The Rule of 72 calculates how fast a market share can be doubled, assuming a constant rate of annual growth.

Directions: For each of the following items, decide which choice best completes the statement. Write the letter that identifies your choice on the answer line.

______ 8. The concept that people who live in the same physical area might have the same wants and needs is the basis for
A. demographic market segmentation.
B. psychographic market segmentation.
C. geographic segmentation.
D. all of the above

______ 9. Your interests and values are identified by
A. demographic market segmentation.
B. psychographic market segmentation.
C. geographic segmentation.
D. product usage market segmentation.

______10. Market segments can be evaluated by
A. the ability to communicate with consumers through the promotional mix.
B. geographic location.
C. the number of brands sold.
D. all of the above

Activity 1 • Identifying Market Segments

Directions: Markets are segmented because marketers want to direct their marketing strategies to consumers who are willing and able to make purchases. All types of segments can be located, even within a fairly homogeneous group of people such as students in your school.

For this project, identify ten distinct market segments in your school and at least one product or service that can be marketed to each. To get you started, one example has been given.

Market Segment	Product/Service
1. Juniors	Class ring
2.	
3.	
4.	
5.	
6.	
7.	
8.	
9.	
10.	

Activity 2 • Global Market Segments

Directions: Some products that sell well in one country do not sell well in another county. Investigate the companies listed below. Describe the problems they faced when they began to move into global markets.

1. McDonald's

____

____

____

____

____

2. Coca-Cola

____

____

____

____

____

3. Nestle

____

____

____

____

 ©South-Western Publishing

Lesson 7.2 Positioning for Competitive Advantage
LESSON QUIZ

Directions: For each of the following statements, if the statement is true, write a T on the answer line; if the statement is false, write an F on the answer line.

______ 1. Positioning highlights differences between competitors in the mind of the consumer.

______ 2. The only way to position a product is to highlight a feature or attribute that it possesses.

______ 3. Information is collected about your household every time you use a frequent shopper or loyalty card.

______ 4. Marketers may try to convince consumers that a single product can be used in several different ways.

______ 5. Marketers never tried to associate a personality with a product.

______ 6. Promotions have only short-term effects on consumer buying.

______ 7. All businesses need to develop a positioning strategy.

Directions: For each of the following items, decide which choice best completes the statement. Write the letter that identifies your choice on the answer line.

______ 8. Manufacturers can increase their profit by
    A. raising the price of a product.
    B. reducing the cost of materials used to make the product.
    C. reducing the size of the package sold to consumers.
    D. all of the above

______ 9. A business will do well when consumers perceive the attributes of its product as being
    A. expensive.
    B. close to the consumers' ideal image.
    C. cheap.
    D. of average quality.

______10. The business environment includes
    A. new products on the market.
    B. negative publicity.
    C. new technology.
    D. all of the above

Activity 1 • Marketing Positions

Directions: Marketers work very hard to position their products or stores in consumers' minds. They continually strive to create a special image of their products, services, or businesses to set themselves apart from everyone else.

You carry these images in your mind without consciously thinking of them. In the chart, write a specific product or business in your community that refers to the general product category. In the next column, write your image of that product or business. In the last column, write the basis for positioning you believe the marketer used to create that image in your mind.

To get you started, the first one is completed for you. The last three general product categories are blank. Think of a product or business that creates an image in your mind and complete the remaining information.

General Product Category	Specific Product or Business	Image	Basis for Positioning and Image
Cola	Pepsi	For young people	Product user
Grocery store			
Discount store			
Cookies			
Yogurt			
Specialty clothing store			
Athletic shoes			

Lesson 7.3 Competing for Market Segments
LESSON QUIZ

Directions: For each of the following statements, if the statement is true, write a T on the answer line; if the statement is false, write an F on the answer line.

______ 1. Businesses face different types of competition when positioning their products.

______ 2. Direct competition is competition between businesses in the same location.

______ 3. Indirect competition occurs when two brands of similar products are compared.

______ 4. Investors expect businesses that operate on the Internet to earn a profit like the more traditional businesses.

______ 5. Consumers have limited dollars to spend on each product or service.

______ 6. The consumer benefits from competition between businesses.

______ 7. Competition limits the variety of products that are available.

Directions: For each of the following items, decide which choice best completes the statement. Write the letter that identifies your choice on the answer line.

______ 8. Rivalry among firms on the basis of price and value is called
    A. direct competition.
    B. indirect competition.
    C. price competition.
    D. all of the above

______ 9. Every company wants to make its products
    A. more expensive.
    B. distinctive.
    C. less expensive.
    D. all of the above

______10. Competition creates products that
    A. are better than existing products.
    B. meet the needs of consumers.
    C. meet the wants of consumers.
    D. all of the above

Activity 1 • Learning About Your Competition—Pricing Strategies

Directions: Each business has its own pricing strategy based on its marketing mix. For each of the following, determine the price of the product/service by telephoning, visiting the store, or reading advertisements. Use stores in your own community. Locate at least five prices for each product. Write the name of the business in the upper cell and write the price in the lower cell for each item.

	Business/Price #1	Business/Price #2	Business/Price #3	Business/Price #4	Business/Price #5
Men's haircut					
16 oz. Bottle of shampoo (select the brand)					
Candy bar (Choose brand.)					
Car oil change					
Digital camera					

Directions: Select two of the products or services and illustrate your findings with either a bar graph or a line graph. Make sure you record the price and the store where you obtained the information.

 ©South-Western Publishing

Lesson 7.4 Learning About the Competition
LESSON QUIZ

Directions: For each of the following statements, if the statement is true, write a T on the answer line; if the statement is false, write an F on the answer line.

______ 1. The marketing mix is developed to meet the wants and needs of a company's consumers.

______ 2. The pricing strategies of your direct competition are valuable knowledge for your business.

______ 3. Outdoor advertising has become less popular in recent years.

______ 4. A competitor's market position does not affect the company's success.

______ 5. Competitors willingly exchange essential information.

______ 6. Your salespeople can discover information about your competitors' products and prices.

______ 7. Trade shows are a good source of information about your competition.

Directions: For each of the following items, decide which choice best completes the statement. Write the letter that identifies your choice on the answer line.

______ 8. If you have information about your competitor's promotional strategies, you can
    A. counter with a strategy to keep your business competitive.
    B. lower your prices.
    C. offer more products.
    D. use the same strategy.

______ 9. You can gain information about your competitor's marketing strategy by
    A. reading the sports section in the newspaper.
    B. shopping in the competitor's business.
    C. visiting the library.
    D. all of the above

______10. The process of gaining competitive market information is called
    A. marketing intelligence.
    B. business research.
    C. competitive analysis.
    D. information gathering.

Activity 1 • Make a Billboard

Directions: You probably pass several billboards on your way to class. Some may be creative enough to catch your attention. Design a billboard that will interest commuters on their way to or from work or class.

Explain your design.

____

____

____

____

Activity 2 • Never Too Much

Directions: Billboards aren't the only kind of outdoor advertising. Bus benches, fences, and other outdoor objects can become outdoor advertising. Design a bus bench that will accompany your billboard.

Lesson 8.1 What Is E-Commerce?
LESSON QUIZ

Directions: For each of the following statements, if the statement is true, write a T on the answer line; if the statement is false, write an F on the answer line.

______ 1. Many established businesses use e-commerce to conduct business.

______ 2. E-commerce includes only sales made on the Internet.

______ 3. All businesses could complete all business activities using the Internet.

______ 4. Businesses go through three stages as they develop their e-commerce presence on the Internet.

______ 5. Businesses on the Internet have immediate access to prospective customers all over the world.

______ 6. There are no disadvantages for businesses operating on the Internet.

______ 7. The Internet has resulted in the development of new products that can be delivered to customers' computers.

Directions: For each of the following items, decide which choice best completes the statement. Write the letter that identifies your choice on the answer line.

______ 8. Around the world, the Internet is used by
   A. 10,000 people.
   B. 500,000 people.
   C. 50 million people.
   D. 500 million people.

______ 9. A business that performs almost all of its business activities through the Internet is referred to as a
   A. dot.com business.
   B. web.com business.
   C. bricks and mortar business.
   D. traditional business.

______ 10. The most basic web site
   A. provides interaction.
   B. provides information.
   C. provides sales transactions.
   D. all of the above

Activity 1 • Business Information

Directions: The Internet is an excellent source of information about businesses, regardless if they operate on the Internet or not. Sometimes, you will find information on a web site created by the company. Other times, you will find information about a specific company on a web site created by other businesses. These businesses may provide information for potential investors or customers. For the companies listed below, identify a web site that provides information about the company and describe the information you found about the business, its products, or its history.

1. Burger King – Web site address:____

____

____

____

____

2. LensCrafters – Web site address:____

____

____

____

____

3. John Deere – Web site address:____

____

____

____

____

Activity 2 • Identifying E-Commerce Stages

Directions: Visit the web sites for the five companies listed below. Identify the web address for the business, describe a few features of the site, and identify the stage of development for the company's web activities.

Business	Internet Address	Web Site Features	Stage
Pizza Hut			
Procter & Gamble			
DIRECTV			
Pepsico			
Dell Computer			

Lesson 8.2 The Growing Importance of E-Commerce
LESSON QUIZ

Directions: For each of the following statements, if the statement is true, write a T on the answer line; if the statement is false, write an F on the answer line.

_______ 1. The Internet was developed as a military and research tool in the 1970s.

_______ 2. In 2000, China had more Internet users than any other country in the world.

_______ 3. Internet sales to consumers represent less than one percent of all consumer purchases.

_______ 4. Many businesses believe that the Internet is not useful for the type of business activities they perform.

_______ 5. Businesses can use the Internet to distribute information to customers but not to employees.

_______ 6. The Internet has not affected a company's ability to find information about its customers.

_______ 7. Small businesses can benefit competitively from using the Internet.

Directions: For each of the following items, decide which choice best completes the statement. Write the letter that identifies your choice on the answer line.

_______ 8. From the very beginning of the Internet, the primary way people have communicated using Internet technology is through
   A. web pages.
   B. commercial transactions.
   C. e-mail.
   D. all of the above

_______ 9. A business can use the information it gathers to
   A. improve its marketing mix.
   B. reorganize its structure.
   C. construct new offices.
   D. choose its officers.

_______10. Businesses that do not provide information about themselves on the Internet
   A. may miss some potential customers.
   B. will fail.
   C. will not develop new technology.
   D. all of the above

Activity 1 • Communicating on the Internet

Directions: A domain name is part of a web address used to identify a common characteristic of a group of web addresses. A domain name for a business usually contains the name of the business and an extension or suffix that identifies the common characteristic of the group of users. For example, Microsoft has the domain name microsoft.com. The most common domain extensions, considered to be top-level domain names, are .com, .net, .gov, .org, .mil, and .edu. A number of other extensions are used to identify the country where the business or web site originates. For example, a business operating in the United Kingdom may use the extension .uk. Complete the following chart by identifying the extension and the meaning of the extension. Some information has been provided for you.

Group/Country	Extension/Suffix	Meaning	Group/Country	Extension/Suffix	Meaning
Top-level domain name	.com		Portugal		
Top-level domain name	.edu		Norway		
Top-level domain name	.gov		Japan		
Top-level domain name	.mil		Spain		
Top-level domain name	.org		Ireland		
Top-level domain name	.net		Italy		
China			France		
Greece			Australia		
Zambia			Egypt		
Thailand			Jamaica		
Sweden			Zimbabwe		

Lesson 8.3 Impact of E-Commerce on Distribution Channels
LESSON QUIZ

Directions: For each of the following statements, if the statement is true, write a T on the answer line; if the statement is false, write an F on the answer line.

_______ 1. Consumers have more choices of companies and products as a result of the Internet.

_______ 2. Eventually, U.S. consumers will make up only a small percentage of individuals shopping on the Internet.

_______ 3. The Internet has made it easier for a company to process an order.

_______ 4. An electronic order is filled incorrectly more often than an order placed in person.

_______ 5. All purchases require that an item be physically shipped to the customer.

_______ 6. Cookies can be sent to a consumer's computer and stored there with or without their permission.

_______ 7. There are alternatives to using a credit card to purchasing a product on the Internet.

Directions: For each of the following items, decide which choice best completes the statement. Write the letter that identifies your choice on the answer line.

_______ 8. Consumers can easily find suppliers and vendors on the Internet by
   A. randomly visiting several web sites.
   B. entering the web address of a specific supplier.
   C. looking at the library.
   D. using a search engine.

_______ 9. Which of the following products can be electronically delivered to a customer?
   A. flowers
   B. bicycles
   C. books
   D. all of the above

_______10. Which of the following products can be electronically ordered by a customer?
   A. flowers
   B. bicycles
   C. books
   D. all of the above

Activity 1 • Comparison Shopping

Directions: Use a search engine on the Internet to identify three suppliers of each of the following products. Visit each site and identify the price for identical or very similar products. Select one of the vendors and explain the reasons for your choice.

	Business/Price #1	Business/Price #2	Business/Price #3	Business/reasons for choice
One dozen roses				
Tricycle				
Bird feeder				
Music CD				
Halloween costume				

Activity 2 • Cookie Jar

Directions: On your computer system, cookies likely are stored in the directory C:\\Windows\Cookies. Identify the cookies that were most recently added to your system. Enter the name of the cookie, the date the cookie was added, and the name of the business that sent the cookie.

Cookie	Date	Business

  ©South-Western Publishing

Lesson 8.4 Role of Promotion for E-Commerce
LESSON QUIZ

Directions: For each of the following statements, if the statement is true, write a T on the answer line; if the statement is false, write an F on the answer line.

______ 1. Most Internet users do not plan to purchase products when they go online.

______ 2. Many consumers will gather information online, then make the actual purchase at a local business.

______ 3. Many companies use bartering to place their advertisements on another web site.

______ 4. The Bureau of Internet Art has set standards for the size and appearance of Internet advertisements.

______ 5. It is not possible to obtain unbiased consumer information about products on the Internet.

______ 6. Web sites sponsored by companies and organizations always charge fees to their prospective customers.

______ 7. Internet shoppers are less satisfied with their online shopping experience than with the other ways they make purchases.

Directions: For each of the following items, decide which choice best completes the statement. Write the letter that identifies your choice on the answer line.

______ 8. To move business activities online, businesses will need to
A. purchase equipment.
B. develop procedures.
C. train personnel.
D. all of the above

______ 9. Internet advertising is measured in
A. web pages.
B. pixels.
C. hits.
D. inches.

______10. Features likely to increase online purchasing include
A. close-up images of products.
B. a large number of web pages.
C. detailed descriptions of products.
D. all of the above

Activity 1 • Internet Advertisements

Directions: The consumers who choose to visit a particular site can be placed in a market segment. Based on this segmentation, advertisers will choose to place advertisements on sites that attract the same market segment they have chosen. Visit three web sites you normally visit. Record the advertisers on the site, describe the market segment, and explain why the advertisers selected this site.

1. Web site address:________________________   Segment:_____________________________

   Advertiser:____

   Reason:____

   ____

   ____

2. Web site address:________________________   Segment:_____________________________

   Advertiser:____

   Reason:____

   ____

   ____

3. Web site address:________________________   Segment:_____________________________

   Advertiser:____

   Reason:____

   ____

   ____

Activity 2 • Banner Advertisement

Directions: Like traditional advertisements, Internet ads are designed to attract a specific market segment that will be interested in their products. Identify a product and market segment. Draw an Internet banner advertisement that would attract the selected consumers and explain your choices in the design.

Product:_______________________________   Segment:_____________________________

Reason:____

____

____

　　　©South-Western Publishing　　　

Lesson 9.1 Developing a Market Strategy
LESSON QUIZ

Directions: For each of the following statements, if the statement is true, write a T on the answer line; if the statement is false, write an F on the answer line.

_______ 1. A market includes all of the consumers a business would like to serve.

_______ 2. Each market is composed of no more than five segments.

_______ 3. Segments of a market can be identified that have one or more strong needs or wants in common.

_______ 4. A segment can be identified by the way customers make purchase decisions.

_______ 5. A target market can consist of only one market segment.

_______ 6. Businesses will select the market segment that offers the best marketing opportunity to become the target market.

_______ 7. A business can have more than one target market at the same time.

Directions: For each of the following items, decide which choice best completes the statement. Write the letter that identifies your choice on the answer line.

_______ 8. Marketing information systems and marketing research are used to gather information to
A. move products to a storage unit.
B. divide markets into segments.
C. divide market segments into markets.
D. separate the business from consumers.

_______ 9. An effective target market must be
A. large enough to support the business.
B. composed of people who can be identified and located based on existing information.
C. composed of individuals with a wide variety of characteristics.
D. all of the above

______10. Each target market requires marketing activities
A. that are different from other target markets.
B. that are the same as other target markets.
C. that are based on the needs of the business.
D. that meet the responses of every individual in the market segment.

Activity 1 • Segmenting Your Class

Directions: Using your classroom as a sample, survey your classmates and divide the market, consisting of the entire class, into smaller segments using the criteria listed below. Describe each segment.

1. Based on demographic characteristics – Number of segments:_______________________________

Segment 1	Segment 2	Segment 3	Segment 4

2. Based on psychographic characteristics for the type of music students enjoy and the types of sports they enjoy – Number of segments: ____

Segment 1	Segment 2	Segment 3	Segment 4

3. Based on their attitudes about school, the importance of grades, time spent out of school studying, and the value of post-secondary education – Number of segments: _____________________________

Segment 1	Segment 2	Segment 3	Segment 4

4. Prepare a graph that illustrates one of the segmentation methods.

Activity 2 • Selling To A Segment

Directions: Select a product and choose a target market from the market segments described in Activity 1. Describe why the product and target segment fit together.

Target Segment: _________________ Product: _____________________________________

____

____

____

____

____

____

____

Lesson 9.2 Assessing Marketing Mix Alternatives
LESSON QUIZ

Directions: For each of the following statements, if the statement is true, write a T on the answer line; if the statement is false, write an F on the answer line.

______ 1. In some cases, the target market wants only the basic product.

______ 2. Features can be added to a basic product to make it unique.

______ 3. Customers are always given choices about the product features they will accept.

______ 4. Services provided with a product may make the product easier for consumers to use.

______ 5. Packaging should never be used to attract attention to a product.

______ 6. There are few business decisions that affect distribution.

______ 7. A business should charge the highest price consumers will pay for a product or service.

Directions: For each of the following items, decide which choice best completes the statement. Write the letter that identifies your choice on the answer line.

______ 8. Products aimed at a large market tend to be very
    A. similar.
    B. unique.
    C. expensive.
    D. inexpensive.

______ 9. When customers see few differences between products, they're more likely to choose a product based on
    A. quality.
    B. brand name.
    C. price.
    D. convenience.

______10. Products can be differentiated based on
    A. features.
    B. packaging.
    C. guarantee.
    D. all of the above

Activity 1 • Improving Market Appeal

Directions: Examine items you have purchased recently, products at a local retailer, or products available from an online retailer. Determine an improvement that could be made to the product element of the marketing mix. Describe how these changes will improve the market appeal for the target market.

Product 1	Features	Options
	Services	Brand Name
	Packaging	Guarantee
	Uses	Affect on Target Market
Product 2	Features	Options
	Services	Brand Name
	Packaging	Guarantee
	Uses	Affect on Target Market

   ©South-Western Publishing   Chapter 9

Lesson 9.3 Analyzing Product Purchase Classifications
LESSON QUIZ

Directions: For each of the following statements, if the statement is true, write a T on the answer line; if the statement is false, write an F on the answer line.

_______ 1. There are some products a consumer would not consider buying.

_______ 2. Consumers actively shop for impulse goods.

_______ 3. The purchase of a staple good is important because you use the product often.

_______ 4. Most of the major purchases made by consumers are shopping goods.

_______ 5. Toothpaste may be a specialty good.

_______ 6. Shopping goods must always be sold in the most convenient location.

_______ 7. Businesses that successfully sell unsought goods use a target market strategy.

Directions: For each of the following items, decide which choice best completes the statement. Write the letter that identifies your choice on the answer line.

_______ 8. Products or services that are purchased as a result of an urgent need are
   A. staple goods.
   B. impulse goods.
   C. emergency goods.
   D. shopping goods.

_______ 9. An example of an impulse good is
   A. expensive jewelry.
   B. a bicycle.
   C. a piano.
   D. candy.

_______ 10. Specialty goods
   A. are always expensive.
   B. inspire strong brand loyalty.
   C. are not items a consumer actively shops to purchase.
   D. all of the above

Activity 1 • Mastering Product/Service Classifications

Directions: Using the definitions of the categories, indicate a product/service for each classification based on YOUR purchase behavior.

CLASSIFICATION	PRODUCT/SERVICE
Convenience staple goods	______________________________
Convenience impulse goods	______________________________
Convenience emergency goods	______________________________
Specialty goods	______________________________
Attribute-based shopping goods	______________________________
Price-based shopping goods	______________________________
Unsought goods	______________________________

Directions: After you complete your list, compare it with a classmate's list and answer the following questions.

Why are your lists different? ____

____

____

What products or services were listed in two or more classifications? ______________

____

____

Why did that happen? ____

____

____

Are the same brand names important to everyone? ____________________________

____

____

Why or why not? ____

____

____

　©South-Western Publishing　

Lesson 9.4 Planning for Marketing
LESSON QUIZ

Directions: For each of the following statements, if the statement is true, write a T on the answer line; if the statement is false, write an F on the answer line.

______ 1. Marketing strategies are based on a complete study of a market and the ways the business can serve the market.

______ 2. Speed can determine marketing success in global marketing.

______ 3. It is impossible to determine in advance that a marketing strategy can be implemented as it was planned.

______ 4. A marketing plan usually projects plans for the next five years.

______ 5. There is no relationship between a marketing strategy and a marketing plan.

______ 6. It isn't necessary to gather information from outside the company before preparing a marketing plan.

______ 7. A business needs to know how customers perceive the business and its competitors.

Directions: For each of the following items, decide which choice best completes the statement. Write the letter that identifies your choice on the answer line.

______ 8. A marketing plan is based on
   A. a marketing strategy.
   B. the product.
   C. the market.
   D. the consumer.

______ 9. Developing a marketing plan encourages the marketer to
   A. make decisions about the product.
   B. modify the corporate structure.
   C. determine what competitors are likely to do.
   D. all of the above.

______10. Marketing planning requires
   A. time.
   B. information.
   C. people who understand planning procedures.
   D. all of the above

Activity 1 • Marketing Planning = Marketing Information

Directions: A useful marketing plan begins with information. Explain how a marketing plan can use the environmental information gathered by a marketing information system. To get you started, the first environmental factor has been analyzed.

MARKETING PLAN SECTION	TYPE OF INFORMATION	HOW IT IS USED
Economy	G.N.P., unemployment rate, recession, recovery, discretionary income, salaries	Invest in new product? Raise prices? Buying new equipment/land? Hire new employees? Change marketing mix?
Laws & Regulations		
Costs		
Competition		
Technology		
Social Factors		

Activity 2 • Plan a Trip

Directions: You are planning a vacation in San Diego. You will drive to San Diego and stay for three days before driving home. Complete the following information to help you plan your vacation.

Miles to drive: _______________________ Cost of gasoline: _______________________

Hotel in San Diego: _______________________ Cost of room: _______________________

Number of meals: _______________________ Cost of meals: _______________________

Activities in San Diego: _______________________

Cost of activities: _______________________

Additional expenses: _______________________ Total cost of vacation: _______________________

 ©South-Western Publishing

Lesson 9.5 Developing a Marketing Plan
LESSON QUIZ

Directions: For each of the following statements, if the statement is true, write a T on the answer line; if the statement is false, write an F on the answer line.

______ 1. A mission statement identifies the financial goals of the business.

______ 2. The review of current marketing efforts includes an identification of the markets in which the company hopes to operate in the coming year.

______ 3. Marketers use eye-tracking research to gauge the effectiveness of advertisements and displays.

______ 4. A marketing plan should include information about the current economy.

______ 5. The marketing strategy will clearly identify the target market to be served.

______ 6. If more than one market is identified as a target market, they must respond to the identical marketing mix.

______ 7. The first section of the marketing plan identifies the actions needed to accomplish and evaluate the marketing strategy.

Directions: For each of the following items, decide which choice best completes the statement. Write the letter that identifies your choice on the answer line.

______ 8. Information about your competitors should include the
  A. name of the chief operating officer.
  B. location of the business.
  C. age of the business.
  D. strengths of the business.

______ 9. The strengths and weaknesses of your business
  A. do not belong in a marketing plan.
  B. are determined by reviewing performance in existing markets.
  C. are not important to developing marketing strategies.
  D. do not affect your marketing plan.

______10. The most important part of the marketing plan, in terms of the company's success, is the
  A. information gathered to create the marketing plan.
  B. development of a marketing strategy.
  C. input from the company's officers.
  D. review of the current status.

Activity 1 • Developing a Plan

Directions: As a marketing student you have just learned the importance of planning and how to write a marketing plan. You currently work for a small neighborhood grocery store. Though the owner, J. R. Knight, has operated the business successfully for 25 years, he does not know a great deal about marketing or developing a marketing plan. Recently, the business has faced increasing competition from a new convenience store and a large supermarket located in a shopping center.

You believe that if the owner defined his target market, made marketing mix decisions, and analyzed his business situation, the business could be more profitable. You have decided to tell J. R. Knight about writing a marketing plan.

1. Prepare a presentation to J. R. Knight describing a marketing plan and its value to the business.

2. Develop two charts or other visuals to support your presentation.

3. Be prepared to make your presentation to the class.

Activity 2 • Evaluating Results

Directions: A marketing plan is useful only if the results can be evaluated. If they can't be evaluated, the business will not know what works and what does not work. Therefore, it is important that the mix elements can be measured. Read the following case and help the restaurant owner measure and analyze the results of the marketing plan.

The owner of an Italian restaurant was reviewing sales records and realized that sales were slow for the dinner time on Monday through Thursday. The restaurant seats 100 people. Records indicated that an average of 150 customers was served each night and the average price of a dinner was $11.

The owner decided that in order to increase sales the restaurant would attempt to focus on a specific target market each day of the week. To support this, a promotional campaign was developed with a supporting marketing mix to advertise special days.

Monday—Kids Eat Free!
Tuesday—Senior Citizens—20% discount
Wednesday—Early Bird Special—15% discount on all meals served before 6:00
Thursday—Late nite special!—15% discount on all meals served after 8:00

1. Here are the results after the first week of the advertised specials. Calculate the average meal price each night based on gross sales.

Day	Customers	Gross Sales	Average Meal Price
Monday	350 customers (of which 105 were children)	$3,430	
Tuesday	190 customers (of which 95 were senior citizens)	1,919	
Wednesday	220 customers (of which 85 dined before 6:00)	2,464	
Thursday	260 customers (of which 130 dined after 8:00)	2,730	

2. Evaluate the effectiveness of each promotion and write a recommendation as to which should be continued. ____

____

3. What additional information would be useful to the owner to plan a new marketing strategy? ________

____

____

 ©South-Western Publishing

Lesson 10.1 What Is a Product?
LESSON QUIZ

Directions: For each of the following statements, if the statement is true, write a T on the answer line; if the statement is false, write an F on the answer line.

______ 1. The physical characteristics of a product are not important.

______ 2. McDonald's sells different products in different countries.

______ 3. When choosing a restaurant, consumers think only of the menu.

______ 4. Distributing free samples is one method of familiarizing people with new products.

______ 5. The failure rate for new products is very low.

______ 6. A product will be successful if it meets consumer needs better than other choices.

______ 7. Marketing should not be involved in product development.

Directions: For each of the following items, decide which choice best completes the statement. Write the letter that identifies your choice on the answer line.

______ 8. To interest a consumer, a product must be
    A. useful and meet the consumers' needs.
    B. physically attractive.
    C. reasonably priced.
    D. all of the above

______ 9. Consumer needs should be defined by
    A. marketers.
    B. businesses.
    C. consumers.
    D. all of the above.

______ 10. A market that is often misunderstood by businesses is the
    A. family market.
    B. senior citizen market.
    C. children's market.
    D. teenage market.

Activity 1 • Birthday Party

Directions: Your nephew is turning seven next month. You want to hold a birthday party for him and his 25 classmates. Make a list of the factors that will influence your choice of a location. Identify several locations that could meet your needs. Describe the facilities, entertainment, and price of each business that provides a party location. Explain why you would choose one business over the other.

1. Factors: ____
   ____

2. Business: _______________________ Description: _______________________

   Business: _______________________ Description: _______________________

   Business: _______________________ Description: _______________________

   Business: _______________________ Description: _______________________

3. Selection: _______________________
   Reasons: ____
   ____

Activity 2 • Product Improvement

Directions: Many ideas for product improvements come from discussions with customers. Interview a family member or friend. Discuss a product the consumer recently purchased. Ask questions about the product's appearance and performance. Discuss any problems experienced with the product. Ask for suggestions for possible improvements.

Product	Evaluation/Problems	Suggestions

Lesson 10.2 Components of a New Product
LESSON QUIZ

Directions: For each of the following statements, if the statement is true, write a T on the answer line; if the statement is false, write an F on the answer line.

______ 1. A guarantee is a way to make a product different from other products.

______ 2. Businesses have many choices in the development of new products.

______ 3. Every product can be complex and unique.

______ 4. The most important part of a product is the basic physical product.

______ 5. Most basic products are very much like those of the competitors.

______ 6. Differences in quality can be used to develop a product line.

______ 7. Increasing a product line adds cost to manufacturing.

Directions: For each of the following items, decide which choice best completes the statement. Write the letter that identifies your choice on the answer line.

______ 8. The best possible product is made by
   A. giving demonstrations.
   B. product planning.
   C. consumer preferences.
   D. adding features.

______ 9. A business can be sued when
   A. a product is poorly designed and causes injury.
   B. workers feel they have been discriminated against.
   C. a product breaks and causes injury.
   D. all of the above

______ 10. The basic product
   A. responds to an important need of consumers.
   B. is not changed by enhancements.
   C. should not be improved.
   D. all of the above

Activity 1 • Product Components

Directions: Select a common product such as a toaster or a clock. List several varieties of the product you can purchase at the store. Identify the function of the basic product. List features of each variety that makes it unique.

Product Variety 1: _______________________________________

Product Description	Features
	•
	•
	•
	•

Product Variety 2: _______________________________________

Product Description	Features
	•
	•
	•
	•

Product Variety 3: _______________________________________

Product Description	Features
	•
	•
	•
	•

Lesson 10.3 Product Market Classifications
LESSON QUIZ

Directions: For each of the following statements, if the statement is true, write a T on the answer line; if the statement is false, write an F on the answer line.

______ 1. Marketers develop more effective products when they understand how consumers shop for them.

______ 2. Businesses and organizations make purchase decisions on the basis of derived demand.

______ 3. Most supplies are not uniquely developed for one business.

______ 4. The price of raw materials does not affect the price the company charges for its finished products.

______ 5. Component parts have been either partially or totally processed by another company.

______ 6. Products are sold to either a consumer market or a business market but not both.

______ 7. The classification system for consumer markets is very useful to marketers as they complete product planning.

Directions: For each of the following items, decide which choice best completes the statement. Write the letter that identifies your choice on the answer line.

______ 8. The quantity of a product or service needed to meet the needs of the consumer is the
A. consumer market.
B. direct demand.
C. product classification.
D. primary market.

______ 9. The product/service classification system is based on
A. the importance of the purchase to the consumer.
B. the consumers' willingness to shop at different locations.
C. the consumers' willingness to compare products before buying.
D. all of the above

______10. Capital equipment includes
A. furniture.
B. paper clips.
C. land.
D. all of the above

Activity 1 • Classifications

Directions: Classifications provide a method of organizing a variety of products and other items. For example, books can be classified as fiction, nonfiction, mystery, romance, and autobiographies. Identify several items that are classified and list several classes.

Item: ___________________________   Classes: ___________________________

Item: ___________________________   Classes: ___________________________

Item: ___________________________   Classes: ___________________________

Activity 2 • New Business

Directions: New businesses are constantly being established. Each new business needs a variety of equipment and supplies. Select a new business. Identify and classify the equipment and supplies the business needs to operate.

Business Type: _______________________________

Purchases	Classification

Business Type: _______________________________

Purchases	Classification

Lesson 10.4 Developing Successful New Products
LESSON QUIZ

Directions: For each of the following statements, if the statement is true, write a T on the answer line; if the statement is false, write an F on the answer line.

_______ 1. The Federal Communication Commission regulates how and when the word "new" can be used in advertising.

_______ 2. Most businesses follow a process to identify and develop new products.

_______ 3. Salespeople who work with customers every day have ideas for new products or product improvements.

_______ 4. The easiest step in new product development is usually finding ideas for new products.

_______ 5. Creative thinking exercises can be used to identify product ideas for testing.

_______ 6. To encourage a large number of new product ideas, companies evaluate ideas in the initial development stage.

_______ 7. A prototype will catch errors early in the development process.

Directions: For each of the following items, decide which choice best completes the statement. Write the letter that identifies your choice on the answer line.

_______ 8. A good source of new product ideas is
   A. the encyclopedia.
   B. the newspaper.
   C. problems experienced by customers.
   D. all of the above

_______ 9. After determining that a product idea sounds reasonable, the business will
   A. perform a financial analysis.
   B. develop the product.
   C. market the product.
   D. create and test a sample marketing strategy.

_______10. The last step in product development is
   A. product testing.
   B. introduction into the target market.
   C. building a prototype.
   D. performing a financial analysis.

Activity 1 • Putting It Together

Directions: Product planning does not occur in a vacuum. It is an integral function of marketing that is supported and combined with all other functions to make a business, product, or service successful. Referring to concepts and ideas you have already studied, describe how product planning is affected by each of the following areas. To help you get started the first answer is provided.

1. Marketing concept: *New product ideas should respond to customer needs and create satisfying exchanges between the business and its customers.*

2. Societal concerns:

3. Supply and demand:

4. Global marketplace:

5. Strategic planning:

6. Product positioning:

7. Understanding consumers:

8. The value of research:

9. The relationship to the marketing mix:

10. Marketing planning:

Lesson 11.1 What Are Services?
LESSON QUIZ

Directions: For each of the following statements, if the statement is true, write a T on the answer line; if the statement is false, write an F on the answer line.

______ 1. Services are activities that are intangible.

______ 2. The service industry is growing faster than the goods-producing industry.

______ 3. Advances in technology are leading to automation in several industries.

______ 4. New service areas have opened around the computer industry.

______ 5. Because people cannot touch a service, it is important for the marketer to focus on the physical object the customer receives with the service.

______ 6. Most services can easily be distributed on the Internet.

______ 7. Services should be priced to cover expenses without earning a profit.

Directions: For each of the following items, decide which choice best completes the statement. Write the letter that identifies your choice on the answer line.

______ 8. The goods-producing industry is
   A. growing faster than the service industry.
   B. becoming more automated.
   C. hiring more employees as the industry grows.
   D. all of the above

______ 9. A service is
   A. produced and consumed in different locations.
   B. produced and consumed at different times.
   C. usable after it has been stored.
   D. produced and consumed at the same time.

______10. Services are heterogeneous, meaning they
   A. are consistent.
   B. cost less than tangible goods.
   C. are unique.
   D. are similar, even when produced by different suppliers.

Activity 1 • Creating an Image

Directions: For each of the following services, locate a print, television, or radio advertisement. Determine the basis for the promotion of the service. Record your answers below.

1. Long-distance telephone service
   Type of advertisement: ____
   Message: ____

2. Banking services
   Type of advertisement: ____
   Message: ____

3. Insurance services
   Type of advertisement: ____
   Message: ____

4. Airline services
   Type of advertisement: ____
   Message: ____

5. Financial planning services
   Type of advertisement: ____
   Message: ____

Activity 2 • Service Development

Directions: You have decided to start a home and office cleaning service. Using the steps in new product development, outline the procedures you would go through to develop your service business.

HOME AND OFFICE CLEANING SERVICE

Idea Development: ____

____

Idea Screening: ____

____

Strategy Development: ____

____

Product Development and Testing: ____

____

Product Marketing: ____

____

Describe how planning a service is alike or different from planning a product.

____
____
____
____

Lesson 11.2 Classifying Types and Evaluating Quality
LESSON QUIZ

Directions: For each of the following statements, if the statement is true, write a T on the answer line; if the statement is false, write an F on the answer line.

_______ 1. The development and marketing of services are the same for various types of services.

_______ 2. Many not-for-profit organizations deliver services.

_______ 3. The amount of customer contact a service provider has is another way to classify services.

_______ 4. Equipment-based services can be located anywhere, without any consideration.

_______ 5. Services can be categorized by the level of skill the provider possesses.

_______ 6. The quality of a service is controlled by the consumer.

_______ 7. The quality of a service is evaluated by the consumer.

Directions: For each of the following items, decide which choice best completes the statement. Write the letter that identifies your choice on the answer line.

_______ 8. To develop a viable and appropriate marketing plan, it is helpful for marketers to
   A. try the service for themselves.
   B. sell the service personally.
   C. classify the service.
   D. all of the above

_______ 9. The two types of markets for services are
   A. profit and non-profit markets.
   B. business and individual consumers.
   C. large and small businesses.
   D. retail and wholesale markets.

_______10. Equipment-based services
   A. are labor intensive.
   B. require a large number of service personnel.
   C. are provided with the use of machinery.
   D. all of the above

Activity 1 • The Service Industry Is on the Move

Directions: The service industry in the U.S. economy is growing faster than any other segment of the economy. In order to better understand this growth, research the topic in the library or on the Internet. Use the following questions as guides for your research, but add additional information as appropriate.

1. How many service jobs will be available by the year 2005 or 2010?

2. What type of jobs will be available?

3. What factors are responsible for the rise in the number of service jobs?

Summarize your findings in the following space.

____

____

____

____

____

____

____

____

____

____

____

____

Activity 2 • Service Evaluation

Directions: Design a form that enables customers to evaluate every aspect of your restaurant. Use the following space.

____

____

____

____

____

____

____

____

____

____

____

Lesson 11.3 Developing a Service Marketing Mix
LESSON QUIZ

Directions: For each of the following statements, if the statement is true, write a T on the answer line; if the statement is false, write an F on the answer line.

_______ 1. Services cannot be defined in terms of physical attributes.

_______ 2. Customers pay attention to tangible elements associated with the service.

_______ 3. Many services use endorsements as a promotional strategy.

_______ 4. Word-of-mouth promotion is not important to service providers.

_______ 5. Promotional strategies should appeal to the buying motives of the target market.

_______ 6. The timing of a promotional message is not important.

_______ 7. Speech-recognition software can be trained to recognize industry-specific terminology to translate spoken words and phrases accurately into print.

Directions: For each of the following items, decide which choice best completes the statement. Write the letter that identifies your choice on the answer line.

_______ 8. Many marketers believe that the most powerful promotional tool available is
    A. price reductions.
    B. personal selling.
    C. publicity.
    D. based on the location of the service provider.

_______ 9. The price of a service
    A. can be easily altered.
    B. can be used to improve the market position of the service provider.
    C. can be reduced by bundling.
    D. all of the above

_______ 10. Distribution of a service
    A. never uses intermediaries.
    B. is not important to selling the service.
    C. usually requires only a short channel of distribution.
    D. must be made from a central location.

Activity 1 • Day Care Center

Directions: Day care centers are springing up all over. Since more families have both parents working, the need for day care has risen dramatically. Develop a marketing strategy for the Tiny Tot Day Care Center. Be creative in the choices you make for product/service planning, pricing, promotion, and distribution. Be sure the decisions respond to the characteristics of the target market you identify.

Target Market: ____

____

____

____

Product/Service Management: ____

____

____

____

Pricing: ____

____

____

____

Distribution: ____

____

____

____

Promotion: ____

____

____

____

Activity 2 • Computer Repairs

Directions: You are the new owner/operator of a computer repair store. You have experience repairing computers for a large corporation. You have discovered that there are many consumers, both individuals and businesses, that need computer services. After studying the competition, you discovered that there are few computer repair stores. Armed with this knowledge, you started a small operation in your garage. You hope that it will be a full-time operation and you will be able to become self-employed.

You have very little experience in business operations, but you did take a marketing class in high school. You remember that the key to any successful business is meeting your customers' expectations of quality and service. With this in mind, you have decided to create a one-page brochure to promote your service.

Select the attribute of the service you want to promote and create a one-page advertisement for the business. Make sure the brochure is directed at a specific target market. If possible, use a computer program to create your brochure since you are promoting a computer repair business.

      ©South-Western Publishing   Chapter 11

Lesson 12.1 Business-To-Business Exchange Process
LESSON QUIZ

Directions: For each of the following statements, if the statement is true, write a T on the answer line; if the statement is false, write an F on the answer line.

______ 1. Businesses purchase a variety of services.

______ 2. A producer or manufacturer usually owns everything it needs to develop the products it sells .

______ 3. Businesses purchase products and services needed to operate the business.

______ 4. Diversity programs are designed to increase purchasing from minority-owned firms.

______ 5. Electronic data exchange (EDI) is a cheaper and easier method of handling orders than the Internet.

______ 6. Part of the U.S. military operates like wholesalers and retailers.

______ 7. Having fewer customers means it should be easier to maintain contact with the customers and understand their needs.

Directions: For each of the following items, decide which choice best completes the statement. Write the letter that identifies your choice on the answer line.

______ 8. To market products to businesses, a supplier must
    A. identify the target market.
    B. determine the characteristics and needs of the target market.
    C. develop a marketing mix.
    D. all of the above

______ 9. Businesses that purchase products for resale are
    A. producers.
    B. wholesale and retail businesses.
    C. producers and retailers.
    D. wholesalers and producers.

______ 10. The largest single customer in the world is
    A. the American public.
    B. the U.S. government.
    C. Procter & Gamble Co.
    D. General Motors Corp.

Activity 1 • The U.S. Government Is My Customer

Directions: The U.S. government is one of the largest customers in the world. Identify several suppliers and the products they sell to the government. Include additional information about the business, product, or business relationship. Use current magazines and the Internet to gather the information.

1. Supplier: _________________________________ Product: _________________________________

   Information: ____

   ____

   ____

2. Supplier: _________________________________ Product: _________________________________

   Information: ____

   ____

   ____

3. Supplier: _________________________________ Product: _________________________________

   Information: ____

   ____

   ____

4. Supplier: _________________________________ Product: _________________________________

   Information: ____

   ____

   ____

Activity 2 • Government Contracts

Directions: The Small Business Administration (SBA) helps individuals establish and expand small businesses. It provides financial, technical, and management assistance. The U.S. government often purchases goods and services from small businesses. The Office of Government Contracting and Business Development assists small businesses in applying for government contracts.

Visit the web site for the Office of Government Contracting and Business Development at www.sba.gov/GC/. Use the information at the site or associated sites to describe the process of acquiring business contracts and the type of goods and services involved in government contracting. Explain why a small business would benefit from this assistance.

____

____

____

____

____

____

____

Lesson 12.2 Making Purchasing Decisions in Business
LESSON QUIZ

Directions: For each of the following statements, if the statement is true, write a T on the answer line; if the statement is false, write an F on the answer line.

______ 1. Average cost is the cost per unit.

______ 2. Rather than buying a needed product or service, a business may decide to make it with its own resources.

______ 3. A purchase specification is the level of inventory needed to meet the usage needs of the business until the product can be resupplied.

______ 4. In the case of a modified purchase, other companies may be given the chance to supply the modified product.

______ 5. A purchasing process may become so routine that it is handled by a computer.

______ 6. When the product being purchased is not unique, with many companies offering the same product for sale, repeat purchasing becomes very competitive.

______ 7. The purchasing process ends when the order is placed.

Directions: For each of the following items, decide which choice best completes the statement. Write the letter that identifies your choice on the answer line.

______ 8. The product or service a business purchases will be the one that
    A. has the highest quality.
    B. meets the need at a reasonable price.
    C. has the lowest price.
    D. can be resold to customers.

______ 9. A business making a new purchase must
    A. determine what needs it must meet with the purchase.
    B. decide upon the types of products that can meet their needs.
    C. identify the companies that offer the needed products.
    D. all of the above

______10. Very expensive more important purchases may require the participation of
    A. financial personnel.
    B. lawyers.
    C. one or more members of top management.
    D. all of the above

Activity 1 • Improving Purchasing Procedures

Directions: There are many new ideas about how to improve purchasing procedures. Two of these ideas are total quality management and just-in-time purchasing. Using the library or Internet as resources, prepare a short report on either of these techniques.

Activity 2 • Diagram a Buying Decision

Directions: Assume you are a buyer for a large manufacturer. Develop a flow chart integrating the three types of buying decisions and the steps involved in making business purchases as described in your textbook. A flow chart is a pictorial description of information flowing along a chain of decisions. List each decision in the sequence in which it is made and the possible results. The first decision is shown as an example.

©South-Western Publishing

Lesson 12.3 Making Purchasing Decisions in Business
LESSON QUIZ

Directions: For each of the following statements, if the statement is true, write a T on the answer line; if the statement is false, write an F on the answer line.

_______ 1. The purchasing process followed by a business is simpler and more streamlined than the purchasing process followed by an individual consumer.

_______ 2. The needs of different parts of a business may conflict with each other.

_______ 3. A supplier develops product specifications to clearly describe the product a business needs.

_______ 4. In some businesses, the purchasing department is responsible for maintaining lists of suppliers for various types of products and services.

_______ 5. A purchase order is very detailed to ensure products are supplied in the format and quantity needed at the correct time and price.

_______ 6. When TQM is used in purchasing, employees are not involved in determining what needs to be purchased.

_______ 7. A physical inventory determines the amount of the product on hand by maintaining records of purchases and sales.

Directions: For each of the following items, decide which choice best completes the statement. Write the letter that identifies your choice on the answer line.

_______ 8. An objective rating system used by buyers to compare potential suppliers on important purchasing criteria is
A. supplier rating.
B. vendor analysis.
C. vendor rating.
D. buyer's scale of need.

_______ 9. In business-to-business marketing, the requirements for a purchase are set by the
A. vendor.
B. buyer.
C. arbitrator.
D. marketer.

_______10. A company develops a relationship with its suppliers to keep inventory levels low and to resupply inventory when it is needed in which of the following?
A. just-in-time purchasing
B. total quality management
C. peak supply purchasing
D. inventory processing

Activity 1 • Functional Benefits

Directions: Purchasing is one of the nine marketing functions that is essential for the profitable operation of a business. Using the list provided, indicate how purchasing benefits or relates to each of the remaining functions. The first answer is provided.

Marketing Function	Benefit or Relationship to Purchasing
Selling	Purchasing personnel require information from selling staff to determine what products to purchase and maintain in stock.
Product/Service Management	
Pricing	
Promotion	
Distribution	
Marketing Information Management	
Financing	
Risk Management	

　　　　©South-Western Publishing　　　　

Lesson 12.4 Retail Purchasing
LESSON QUIZ

Directions: For each of the following statements, if the statement is true, write a T on the answer line; if the statement is false, write an F on the answer line.

______ 1. Market conditions for products sold by retailers change very rapidly.

______ 2. Computer technology helps retailers track the sales of current products to determine which products sell rapidly and which do not.

______ 3. The merchandise plan lists the invoices a retailer currently owes for merchandise that has been ordered.

______ 4. A model stock list identifies the minimum amount of important products the store needs to have available to meet the needs of its target market.

______ 5. Retailers purchase items from manufacturers and wholesalers.

______ 6. Only two-thirds of businesses have written ethics policies for purchasing personnel to follow.

______ 7. Large financial losses can occur in businesses that do not have effective procedures for receiving, unpacking, inspecting, and preparing products for sale.

Directions: For each of the following items, decide which choice best completes the statement. Write the letter that identifies your choice on the answer line.

______ 8. The most impersonal type of communication is
   A. a telephone call.
   B. electronic data exchange (EDI).
   C. a fax.
   D. e-mail.

______ 9. Comparison shopping includes a variety of activities such as
   A. examining your competitor's invoices.
   B. determining the services offered by the competitor.
   C. drawing a sample layout of the competitor's store.
   D. identifying the products your competitor currently has in storage.

______10. A retailer's basic stock list
   A. is developed from a merchandise plan.
   B. changes frequently.
   C. will not change much over time.
   D. describes the complete assortment of products a store would like to offer to customers.

Activity 1 • Totaling Totes

Directions: Sue owns a craft store. She needs to reorder tote bags for the fall season. The vendor prices are in the following table.

	Case (4 dozen)	Dozen	Unit
Canvas tote:			
Natural	$ 98.40	$25.08	$2.15
Black, green, navy, red	110.40	28.20	2.41
Nylon fanny pack	122.88	31.44	2.69
Jumbo tote	164.64	42.24	3.60
Zipper tote	159.85	40.92	3.49
Deluxe tote (natural)	153.12	39.25	3.35

Last year, Sue carried only the canvas tote and the deluxe tote. She sold 10 dozen natural canvas totes and 8 3/4 dozen natural deluxe totes. Although she does not do any formal market research, Sue has the following information.

- Sales are up 5 percent from last year.
- This year she has scheduled five craft classes with 12 students per class. Each student will have to purchase a natural canvas tote.

Answer the following questions.

1. How many natural canvas totes does Sue need to order to cover the expected increase in business and the classes? What is the cost of this order?

2. How many natural deluxe totes does she need to order to cover her anticipated sales? What is the cost of this order?

3. What is the total cost for purchasing the natural canvas totes and natural deluxe totes?

4. In addition to the natural totes, Sue also decides to order the following. What is the total cost for this order?

Item	Cost
2 doz. nylon fanny packs	
2 doz. zipper totes	
1 doz. navy canvas totes	
1 doz. black canvas totes	
4 doz. red canvas totes	
4 doz. green canvas totes	
2 doz. jumbo totes	
Total cost	

Lesson 13.1 Marketing through Distribution
LESSON QUIZ

Directions: For each of the following statements, if the statement is true, write a T on the answer line; if the statement is false, write an F on the answer line.

______ 1. Many people and companies are involved in the distribution of products and services from the producer to the consumer.

______ 2. Distribution is essential in a free enterprise economy.

______ 3. A marketer should consider only a single method of distributing a product or service to a target market when developing a marketing strategy or preparing a marketing plan.

______ 4. The success of a product or a business is influenced only by the activities of the business.

______ 5. An important part of marketing is the design and management of an effective distribution system.

______ 6. The producer of a product is not responsible for the distribution method selected for the product.

______ 7. When a product is marketed to a customer, the business must know if special physical handling is needed for the product.

Directions: For each of the following items, decide which choice best completes the statement. Write the letter that identifies your choice on the answer line.

______ 8. The oldest and most basic part of marketing is
   A. distribution.
   B. production.
   C. advertising.
   D. placing an order.

______ 9. The amount of satisfaction a consumer receives from the consumption of a particular product or service is
   A. product satisfaction.
   B. consumption satisfaction.
   C. economic utility.
   D. based solely on distribution.

______10. Businesses that apply the marketing concept will fail if distributors
   A. are not involved in writing the marketing plan.
   B. do not follow the marketing plan.
   C. are opposed to the marketing plan developed by the business.
   D. all of the above

Activity 1 • Distributors Do Marketing

Directions: Review business magazines and newspapers to find stories about businesses and distributors. Identify a specific activity that distributors perform that is related to each of the following marketing functions. Write a brief description of each activity in the space provided.

Selling: ____

____

Promotion: ____

____

Risk reduction: ____

____

Pricing: ____

____

Marketing-information management: ____

____

Product/service management: ____

____

Purchasing: ____

____

Activity 2 • Around the World

Directions: Identify several local manufacturers. Using information from the companies or Internet, determine where the products are distributed and sold.

Manufacturer:_____________________________   Product: ______________________
Sold in:
    Location 1: ____
    Location 2: ____
    Location 3: ____
    Location 4: ____

Manufacturer: ____________________________   Product: ______________________
Sold in:
    Location 1: ____
    Location 2: ____
    Location 3: ____
    Location 4: ____

Manufacturer: ____________________________   Product: ______________________
Sold in:
    Location 1: ____
    Location 2: ____
    Location 3: ____
    Location 4: ____

　　©South-Western Publishing　　

Lesson 13.2 Assembling Channels of Distribution
LESSON QUIZ

Directions: For each of the following statements, if the statement is true, write a T on the answer line; if the statement is false, write an F on the answer line.

_______ 1. Channels of distribution are not required in marketing.

_______ 2. There are no differences in what producers develop and what customers need.

_______ 3. Businesses usually sell their products directly to large numbers of customers who purchase only what they need for personal consumption.

_______ 4. A channel of distribution will accumulate products from a number of manufacturers and make them available in one location to give consumers adequate choice and variety to meet their needs.

_______ 5. A channel of distribution is necessary to move the product from the place where it is produced to the place where it will be consumed.

_______ 6. An indirect channel of distribution is most often selected when consumers are located in a limited geographic area.

_______ 7. A member of a channel of distribution can be considered to be a supplier or a customer.

Directions: For each of the following items, decide which choice best completes the statement. Write the letter that identifies your choice on the answer line.

_______ 8. When products and services are exchanged, they move through
   A. a product pipeline.
   B. a single distributor.
   C. a channel of distribution.
   D. several channels of distribution.

_______ 9. In the exchange between producer and consumer,
   A. only the producer is responsible for completing all of the marketing functions.
   B. only the consumer is responsible for completing all of the marketing functions.
   C. a channel of distribution may be responsible for completing some of the marketing functions.
   D. a channel of production can choose to complete some of the marketing functions.

_______10. The relationship between sales and depletion can be a valuable indicator of
   A. past sales.
   B. the efficiency of the distribution channel.
   C. future sales trends.
   D. current production.

Activity 1 • Local Grocery Store, International Products

Directions: Your local grocery store provides perishable foods and products from farms and other producers around the world. Visit your local grocery store. Select items in each category listed below. Check labels or use the Internet to identify the producer and location where the items were grown or produced. Evaluate the durability of the product by estimating how long it will be edible or usable. Identify any special handling the product may need as it is distributed.

Fresh Fruit

Product: _______________________________ Producer: _______________________________
Durability: _____________________________ Location: _______________________________
Special handling: ____

Product: _______________________________ Producer: _______________________________
Durability: _____________________________ Location: _______________________________
Special handling: ____

Baked Goods

Product: _______________________________ Producer: _______________________________
Durability: _____________________________ Location: _______________________________
Special handling: ____

Product: _______________________________ Producer: _______________________________
Durability: _____________________________ Location: _______________________________
Special handling: ____

Meat

Product: _______________________________ Producer: _______________________________
Durability: _____________________________ Location: _______________________________
Special handling: ____

Product: _______________________________ Producer: _______________________________
Durability: _____________________________ Location: _______________________________
Special handling: ____

Frozen Foods

Product: _______________________________ Producer: _______________________________
Durability: _____________________________ Location: _______________________________
Special handling: ____

Product: _______________________________ Producer: _______________________________
Durability: _____________________________ Location: _______________________________
Special handling: ____

Dairy Products

Product: _______________________________ Producer: _______________________________
Durability: _____________________________ Location: _______________________________
Special handling: ____

Product: _______________________________ Producer: _______________________________
Durability: _____________________________ Location: _______________________________
Special handling: ____

 ©South-Western Publishing

Lesson 13.3 Wholesaling
LESSON QUIZ

Directions: For each of the following statements, if the statement is true, write a T on the answer line; if the statement is false, write an F on the answer line.

_______ 1. Manufacturers produce products only when they are necessary or in season.

_______ 2. A wholesaler combines the orders of several final consumers and purchases in efficient quantities.

_______ 3. A wholesaler may specialize in storage and inventory management.

_______ 4. The typical wholesaling activities include producing, buying, selling, transporting, and storing products.

_______ 5. A wholesaler may finance the inventory of the manufacturer until it can be sold and extend credit to retailers to enable them to make purchases.

_______ 6. Wholesalers are helpful in expanding a manufacturer's market.

_______ 7. Many large retailers refuse to deal with wholesalers.

Directions: For each of the following items, decide which choice best completes the statement. Write the letter that identifies your choice on the answer line.

_______ 8. A wholesaler becomes part of a channel of distribution when
   A. there are too many retailers for a manufacturer to serve efficiently.
   B. a retailer works with a large number of producers.
   C. the wholesaler is able to complete a large number of marketing tasks that manufacturers or retailers do not want to perform.
   D. all of the above

_______ 9. A wholesale club targets
   A. small businesses.
   B. employees of large businesses.
   C. individual customers.
   D. all of the above

_______10. Wholesalers can help a producer
   A. build international business.
   B. sell directly to the final consumer.
   C. prepare a marketing plan.
   D. all of the above

Activity 1 • Moving Potato Chips

Directions: Potato chips are sold by retailers to both final consumers for consumption and business consumers for resale. Connect the appropriate channel members so that each consumer gets potato chips through a logical channel. Be prepared to explain your decisions.

Potato Chip Producer

Distribution Center	Drop Shipper	Rack Jobber

Convenience Stores	Large Grocery Stores	Hospitals	School Cafeterias	Restaurants

Students	Patients	Patrons	Families	Golfers

Activity 2 • Club Members

Directions: Contact a nearby wholesale club or visit the Internet site for Sam's Club or Costco Wholesale. Answer the following questions.

Membership requirements: ____

Membership levels: ____

Cost of membership: ____

Membership benefits: ____

Lesson 13.4 Retailing
LESSON QUIZ

Directions: For each of the following statements, if the statement is true, write a T on the answer line; if the statement is false, write an F on the answer line.

______ 1. The primary customers of a retailer are individual consumers purchasing to meet their own needs.

______ 2. Retailers purchase products only from wholesalers.

______ 3. Retailers store much of the inventory of products until they are purchased by the final customer.

______ 4. All promotion is performed by manufacturers rather than retailers.

______ 5. Shopping strips have between 20 and 30 stores that offer a broad range of products.

______ 6. Retailing changes rapidly.

______ 7. Retail opportunities in the Soviet Union and Africa will expand in the future.

Directions: For each of the following items, decide which choice best completes the statement. Write the letter that identifies your choice on the answer line.

______ 8. Stores can be categorized based on the
  A. characteristics of their customers.
  B. types of products offered.
  C. part of the country where they are located.
  D. name of the store.

______ 9. Non-store retailing includes
  A. specialty stores.
  B. shopping strips.
  C. catalog sales.
  D. all of the above

______10. Franchises are guided by
  A. the franchise plan.
  B. consumers.
  C. the channel of distribution.
  D. all of the above

Activity 1 • Specialty Retailers

Directions: Select a nearby specialty retailer you can visit. Answer the following questions.

Retailer: ____

Product selection: _______________________________________

____

____

____

Target market description: ________________________________

____

____

____

How does the retailer attract its target market? ________________

____

____

Activity 2 • Retail Location

Directions: Location is important to all retailers who expect customers to visit the retail store. Select a nearby retailer and evaluate the following characteristics of its location.

Retailer: _____________________________   Location: _____________________________

Type of retailer: _______________________   Target market: _______________________

Nearby retailers or businesses: ____

Characteristics of the building: ____

Characteristics of the parking area: ____

Amount of automobile traffic: ____

Amount of foot traffic: ____

Traffic patterns (traffic lights, commuters in the morning, etc.):____________________________

____

Accessibility from major roads: ____

Public transportation: ____

Signage: ____

Lesson 13.5 Physical Distribution Keeps Things Moving
LESSON QUIZ

Directions: For each of the following statements, if the statement is true, write a T on the answer line; if the statement is false, write an F on the answer line.

______ 1. Physical distribution includes storage of a product as it moves through the channel of distribution.

______ 2. Products are often grouped into large units for transportation and then divided into smaller units for display and sale.

______ 3. Railroads are particularly useful for carrying a large quantity of small products that need to be delivered quickly.

______ 4. Air transportation is the best choice for delivering products rapidly.

______ 5. A pipeline can be expensive to construct and difficult to maintain.

______ 6. Most products are delivered from the manufacturer to the final customer using a single transportation method.

______ 7. Coal and wood can be transported by pipelines.

Directions: For each of the following items, decide which choice best completes the statement. Write the letter that identifies your choice on the answer line.

______ 8. Factors involved in selecting a transportation method for products include the
    A. location where the product is to be delivered.
    B. type of product to be shipped.
    C. speed of delivery.
    D. all of the above

______ 9. The most flexible major transportation method is
    A. railroads.
    B. trucks.
    C. ships and boats.
    D. air.

______10. The major problem with using ships as a transportation method is
    A. cost.
    B. speed.
    C. the inability to handle large products.
    D. all of the above

Activity 1 • Special Requirements in Distribution

Directions: Pretend you are the grower/manufacturer of fresh flowers, book bags, and tropical birds. Answer the following questions for each product.

1. Where will the product be produced?
2. Where will the product be used?
3. Where will the product be exchanged?
4. What characteristics of the product will affect distribution?
5. What type of special handling is needed?
6. What type of risk is assumed by the distributor?

Fresh flowers:____

____

____

Book bags:____

____

____

Tropical birds:____

____

____

Activity 2 • Trans-Alaska Pipeline

Directions: The Trans-Alaska pipeline provides 17 percent of America's domestic oil production. Use the library or Internet to answer the following questions.

When was the pipeline constructed? ____

When did the first oil move through the pipeline? _____________________________

How long is the pipeline?____

How much of the pipeline is above ground?___________________________________

What is the diameter of the pipe?____

Where does the pipeline start and end?______________________________________

____

How much did it cost to build the pipeline?___________________________________

Why does the pipeline zigzag?____

____

Lesson 14.1 The Economics of Price Decisions
LESSON QUIZ

Directions: For each of the following statements, if the statement is true, write a T on the answer line; if the statement is false, write an F on the answer line.

_______ 1. The lowest price is always the best price for every customer.

_______ 2. Price is an important tool for marketers because it can be changed much more quickly than other marketing decisions.

_______ 3. Price allocates available resources among people.

_______ 4. If sales increase, profits will increase as well.

_______ 5. If you lower the price of your product, you will sell a larger quantity of the product.

_______ 6. In the United States, it is illegal for two companies to agree on the amount they will charge for products or services.

_______ 7. It is illegal for a business to lure a customer into a store by offering a low price and then telling the customer that the low-priced product is unavailable.

Directions: For each of the following items, decide which choice best completes the statement. Write the letter that identifies your choice on the answer line.

_______ 8. Value is added to a product when
    A. it is available in a location that is more convenient for consumers.
    B. it is available during more convenient hours.
    C. it is modified to become more useful.
    D. all of the above

_______ 9. The relationship between changes in a product's price and the demand for that product is known as
    A. equilibrium price.
    B. elastic demand.
    C. economic utility.
    D. price/demand ratio.

_______10. In a private enterprise economy, governments
    A. encourage activities that benefit society.
    B. determine product prices.
    C. prevent companies from growing.
    D. all of the above

Activity 1 • Business Information

Directions: Pricing strategies are used every day by businesses to attract attention and gain customers. Look at a local newspaper and clip five advertisements that use price as part of the promotional strategy. Mount each advertisement on a separate sheet of paper and provide the following information for each ad.

1. Name of the business
2. Item being advertised
3. Target market for this item
4. Type of competition for this item
5. Type of pricing techniques used

Directions: Locate five advertisements that use non-pricing strategies. Clip and mount these ads on separate sheets of paper and provide the following information:

1. Name of the business
2. Item being advertised
3. Target market for this item
4. Type of competition for this item
5. Unique quality of the item that is being advertised

Activity 2 • It's the Law

Directions: Using the library or Internet, research two laws that relate to pricing. Answer the following questions.

Name of the law: ____
   Date the law was enacted: _______________________________________
   Purpose of the law: ____
   ____
   Is the law still in existence? _____________________________________
   Example of how the law helps businesses: ___________________________
   ____
   Example of how the law helps consumers: ___________________________
   ____

Name of the law: ____
   Date the law was enacted: _______________________________________
   Purpose of the law: ____
   ____
   Is the law still in existence? _____________________________________
   Example of how the law helps businesses: ___________________________
   ____
   Example of how the law helps consumers: ___________________________
   ____

     ©South-Western Publishing   Chapter 14

Lesson 14.2 Developing Pricing Procedures
LESSON QUIZ

Directions: For each of the following statements, if the statement is true, write a T on the answer line; if the statement is false, write an F on the answer line.

_______ 1. Companies that want to maximize profits study consumer demand to determine what customers in the target market are willing to pay for their products.

_______ 2. Sales-based pricing objectives result in prices that achieve the highest possible sales volume.

_______ 3. A company that does not post prices with its product is trying to appeal to cost-conscious customers.

_______ 4. A campaign using rebates and coupons cannot increase the company's profits.

_______ 5. A business that charges low prices is creating an image based on low quality.

_______ 6. A company can determine the minimum price by performing a breakeven analysis.

_______ 7. Fixed costs are determined by the quantity of the product that is produced or sold.

Directions: For each of the following items, decide which choice best completes the statement. Write the letter that identifies your choice on the answer line.

_______ 8. The company that wants to maximize profits would usually select
    A. a large target market.
    B. a small target market.
    C. more than one target market.
    D. a target market that is not well defined.

_______ 9. The highest possible price that can be charged is determined by the
    A. costs of the seller.
    B. target market.
    C. government.
    D. marketer.

______10. A high markup
    A. increases the profit a business makes on the product.
    B. increases the quantity sold.
    C. decreases the quantity sold.
    D. reduces costs to the business.

Activity 1 • Calculating Costs

Directions: Use the following information to answer the questions below.

Sierra has opened a small business in her home designing T-shirts. The current selling price is $28.

Costs of Goods Sold for Each Shirt	
Shirts	$8
Related materials	4
Ironing and sewing	2

Monthly Fixed Costs	
Rent	$100
Utilities	30
Transportation	25
Postage	30
Miscellaneous	20

Sales Last Year	
Month	Units Sold
January	15
February	20
March	25
April	50
May	75
June	15
July	18
August	5
September	20
October	250
November	225
December	15

What is Sierra's total revenue?

____

What is the total cost of goods sold?

____

What is the gross margin?

____

What are the total fixed costs?

____

What is Sierra's net profit?

____

What is the break-even point?

____

What is the markup as a percentage of the selling price?

____

What is the markup as a percentage of cost?

____

Lesson 14.3 Pricing Based on Market Conditions
LESSON QUIZ

Directions: For each of the following statements, if the statement is true, write a T on the answer line; if the statement is false, write an F on the answer line.

_______ 1. The type of competition faced by a product changes throughout the stages of its life cycle.

_______ 2. During the introductory stage, only one brand of a new product is available, allowing the business to control the price.

_______ 3. A penetration price usually results in higher profits for the company and encourages other companies to enter the market.

_______ 4. In later stages of the life cycle, competition decreases and there is an emphasis on price competition.

_______ 5. Companies selling products with many similar competitors can be less concerned about the price of competing products or services.

_______ 6. With zone pricing, different product or transportation costs are set for specific areas of the seller's market.

_______ 7. "FOB factory" means the manufacturer will pay all transportation costs from the point where the product is manufactured.

Directions: For each of the following items, decide which choice best completes the statement. Write the letter that identifies your choice on the answer line.

_______ 8. A very high price designed to emphasize the quality or uniqueness of the product is known as the
   A. skimming price.
   B. penetration price.
   C. equilibrium price.
   D. maximum price.

_______ 9. For staple convenience goods,
   A. price competition is fierce.
   B. price is not important to customers.
   C. customers see a great deal of difference between available products.
   D. factors other than price are more important in choosing a product.

_______10. A flexible pricing policy means
   A. prices can be changed quickly.
   B. customers can negotiate a price within a set price range.
   C. all customers pay the same price.
   D. pricing is based on the quantity produced.

Activity 1 • Product Life Cycle

Directions: Create a flow chart that identifies the stages in a product's life cycle. Include a description of sales levels for each stage.

Activity 2 • Pricing and the Product Life Cycle

Directions: The product life cycle helps marketers determine how to price their products based on competition and the uniqueness of the products. Assume your company has developed a new sunscreen that is guaranteed to last all day. It is waterproof, odorless, colorless, and will not wipe off or sting the user's eyes. The following chart identifies what the manufacturer and the competition are doing. For each scenario, determine what stage of the life cycle the sunscreen is in and what type of pricing strategy would be appropriate.

Manufacturer/Competitor	Life-Cycle Stage	Pricing Strategy
Introduce product/no competition	Introduction	Price skimming
Product well-received/ Similar products entering the market		
Many similar products are on the market/No substantial change in your product		
Competition cuts prices/ No substantial change in your product		
A competitor offers a new product that is an effective skin moisturizer with an all-day sunblock and a 50 percent lower price.		

     ©South-Western Publishing

Lesson 15.1 Promotion as a Form of Communication
LESSON QUIZ

Directions: For each of the following statements, if the statement is true, write a T on the answer line; if the statement is false, write an F on the answer line.

______ 1. Consumers remember every promotional message they receive.

______ 2. People will not purchase a good or service until they know its characteristics and benefits.

______ 3. Promotions that inform are used only for new products and services.

______ 4. Encoding is putting a message into language or symbols that are familiar to the sender.

______ 5. Receivers of promotional messages are the customers, clients, or potential consumers of a product or service.

______ 6. Receivers of a promotional message tend to modify the message to reflect their own needs, biases, knowledge, and culture.

______ 7. Impersonal communication is often used in business-to-business marketing.

Directions: For each of the following items, decide which choice best completes the statement. Write the letter that identifies your choice on the answer line.

______ 8. Persuasion is an important task of promotion during the
   A. introductory stage of the product life cycle.
   B. growth stage of the product life cycle.
   C. maturity stage of the product life cycle.
   D. decline stage of the product life cycle.

______ 9. The receiver's reaction or response to the source's message is
   A. noise.
   B. always a purchase.
   C. feedback.
   D. agreement.

______10. The type of communication a marketer chooses for promotion depends on
   A. personal selling.
   B. personal communication.
   C. the characteristics of the intended target market.
   D. mass communication.

Activity 1 • Informing, Persuading, and Reminding

Directions: The purpose of promotion is to inform, persuade, and remind the consumer of products and services. As products move through the product life cycle, marketers use various promotional tools to convey messages to their target audiences. For one of the following products, sketch an informational billboard, a persuasive billboard, and a reminder billboard.

Campbell's soup	contact lenses
Bic pens	Eureka vacuum cleaner

Informational Billboard

Persuasive Billboard

Reminder Billboard

 ©South-Western Publishing Chapter 15

Lesson 15.2 Types of Promotion
LESSON QUIZ

Directions: For each of the following statements, if the statement is true, write a T on the answer line; if the statement is false, write an F on the answer line.

______ 1. Mass media includes television, radio, word-of-mouth, magazines, and newspapers.

______ 2. Advertising can repeat the promotional message many times.

______ 3. Publicity is any nonpaid form of communication about a business or organization.

______ 4. The major advantage of publicity is the goodwill it can create for an organization, product, or service.

______ 5. Advertising is impersonal.

______ 6. Personal selling provides immediate feedback.

______ 7. Sales promotions provide indirect incentives to buy a good or service.

Directions: For each of the following items, decide which choice best completes the statement. Write the letter that identifies your choice on the answer line.

______ 8. The most common type of promotion is
   A. publicity.
   B. advertising.
   C. informational articles.
   D. mass media.

______ 9. The disadvantages of advertising include
   A. its expressive form.
   B. its ability to reach several geographic areas at the same time.
   C. its repetition.
   D. the target audience may not receive the message.

______10. Personal selling
   A. reaches one customer at a time.
   B. provides personal contact between the seller and the customer.
   C. may have a high cost per customer.
   D. all of the above

Activity 1 • Publicity

Directions: Stories about major businesses are often published in local newspapers. Review several recent issues of the newspaper for your community. Locate a story about a business operating in your community. Based on the article, answer the following questions.

1. What is the name of the business? ____

   ____

2. Where does the business operate? ____

   ____

3. What is the good or service produced by the company? _____________________________

   ____

4. What event caused the article? ____

   ____

5. Will this article create goodwill among consumers? _______________________________

   ____

6. Did the company want this information released? Explain._____________________________

   ____

Activity 2 • Sales Promotions

Directions: Use a current publication. Find a sales promotion in the magazine or newspaper. Use the information to answer the following questions.

1. What is the name of the business sponsoring the promotion? ________________________

   ____

2. Where does the business operate? ____

   ____

3. What is the good or service produced by the company? _____________________________

   ____

4. Who is the target market for the good or service? _________________________________

   ____

5. How is the promotion appropriate for the business? _______________________________

   ____

6. Do you think the promotion will increase the company's profits? Explain._______________

   ____

          ©South-Western Publishing   Chapter 15

Lesson 15.3 Mixing the Promotional Plan
LESSON QUIZ

Directions: For each of the following statements, if the statement is true, write a T on the answer line; if the statement is false, write an F on the answer line.

______ 1. Many businesses rely on a single type of promotion.

______ 2. The marketing mix depends on the promotional mix chosen for the product.

______ 3. The target market is critical to selecting an appropriate promotional mix.

______ 4. Marketers determine which promotional elements should be used for the greatest impact and which have the best chance of meeting the company objectives.

______ 5. Publicity is always initiated or approved by the advertiser.

______ 6. The marketer identifies the target market by developing promotional objectives.

______ 7. Before any steps are taken in preparing a promotional plan, the promotional budget must be determined.

Directions: For each of the following items, decide which choice best completes the statement. Write the letter that identifies your choice on the answer line.

______ 8. A marketer needs to develop a specific promotional mix that will reach
   A. other advertisers.
   B. each target market.
   C. specific geographic areas.
   D. all of the above

______ 9. A carefully arranged sequence of promotions designed around a common theme responsive to specific objectives is
   A. a promotional plan.
   B. a marketing plan.
   C. an advertising plan.
   D. a strategic plan.

______10. The success of each promotion is determined by
   A. the number of people reached.
   B. the number of promotions developed.
   C. the effect on business profits.
   D. all of the above

Activity 1 • Coupon Popularity

Directions: The use of coupons is a major sales promotion tool for many manufacturers and retailers. In an effort to determine the effectiveness of coupons, many firms research their use. The following results were obtained from a survey of 746 households regarding consumer attitudes towards coupons.

Response	1988		1992		Change in Attitude (+/-)
Favorable	350	%	417	%	%
Somewhat Favorable	373	%	313	%	%
Somewhat Unfavorable	23	%	16	%	%

1. Calculate the percentage for each category, rounding off to the nearest whole digit. Place the answers in the table.

2. Calculate the percentage increase or decrease for each category for 1988 to 1992. Place the answers in the table.

3. Why do you believe the figures changed from 1988 to 1992?_______________________________

   ____

   ____

4. Do you believe the figures have changed from 1992 to the present? Explain._________________

   ____

   ____

   ____

Activity 2 • Putting It All Together

Directions: The marketing manager must put together an effective promotional plan that meets the organizational objectives and provides feedback on the campaign's success. Select a product or service of your choice and create a promotional plan. Follow the steps of the promotional planning process to ensure that your planning is thorough and focused.

Activity 3 • Effective Publicity

Directions: Imagine that your school has been asked to participate in the local newspaper's special section on "Up with Education." This section will contain articles about various classes offered in your high school. Your teacher asks you to write an article about Marketing Education.

          ©South-Western Publishing

Lesson 16.1 What Is Advertising?
LESSON QUIZ

Directions: For each of the following statements, if the statement is true, write a T on the answer line; if the statement is false, write an F on the answer line.

______ 1. Over the last few decades, the leading advertising medium has been the Internet.

______ 2. Some industries spend more on advertising than others.

______ 3. The cost per view for television advertising is fairly high.

______ 4. Advertising can target a specific audience by customizing the words, graphics, or length of the advertisement.

______ 5. A cease-and-desist order requires an organization to admit guilt or pay fines for deceptive promotional activity.

______ 6. Substantiation requires an organization to support the information it provides in an advertisement.

______ 7. Currently, consumers must watch the advertisements broadcast on television or taped by personal video recorders.

Directions: For each of the following items, decide which choice best completes the statement. Write the letter that identifies your choice on the answer line.

______ 8. The main theme of organizational advertising is
    A. to promote a specific product or service.
    B. to provide information about an available product.
    C. the benefits of the business to customers or society.
    D. all of the above

______ 9. A corrective advertisement
    A. must provide all information necessary for a customer to make a safe and informed decision.
    B. proves the claims made in earlier advertisements.
    C. corrects any false impressions made by earlier advertisements.
    D. all of the above

______10. Self-regulation is provided by
    A. the National Association of Broadcasters.
    B. the Better Business Bureau.
    C. the American Association of Advertising Agencies.
    D. all of the above

Activity 1 • Marketing Activities

Directions: Advertising does not exist in a vacuum. It is an integral part of marketing, which includes nine marketing functions. For each of the following functions, write one statement that shows its relationship to advertising.

Product/service management:____

____

____

Distribution:____

____

____

Pricing:____

____

____

Marketing-information management:____

____

____

Promotion:____

____

____

Financing:____

____

____

Risk management:____

____

____

Selling:____

____

____

Purchasing:____

____

____

Activity 2 • Self-Regulation

Directions: Select one of the self-regulation agencies. Use the library or Internet to investigate the agency. Summarize the results of your research.

Lesson 16.2 Developing an Advertising Plan
LESSON QUIZ

Directions: For each of the following statements, if the statement is true, write a T on the answer line; if the statement is false, write an F on the answer line.

______ 1. An advertising plan is centered on a specific product, service, or group of products and services.

______ 2. The marketing mix should be supported by the advertising objective.

______ 3. Objectives for a specific advertising plan are similar from organization to organization and from product to service.

______ 4. An advertising budget should be developed before the advertising objectives are defined.

______ 5. Spending what you can afford on advertising adequately supports most advertising objectives.

______ 6. A media plan consists of the types of media and the actual media in which advertising will be placed.

______ 7. The reach is the total cost of an advertisement.

Directions: For each of the following items, decide which choice best completes the statement. Write the letter that identifies your choice on the answer line.

______ 8. Each objective in your advertising plan should contain
    A. the advertising message to be communicated.
    B. the identity of your primary competitor.
    C. the cost of obtaining the advertising objective.
    D. all of the above

______ 9. When your advertising budget is determined by the percentage of sales approach,
    A. your advertising budget will always support your advertising objectives.
    B. your advertising budget will be determined by your sales levels.
    C. your budget will consider any new competitive challenges.
    D. all of your advertising tasks will be accomplished.

______10. All advertising messages in a plan should
    A. revolve around a single theme.
    B. be identical.
    C. respond to advertising messages by your competitors.
    D. be coordinated with the receiver.

Activity 1 • Advertising Objectives

Directions: An advertising objective is made up of several parts: (1) the specific message the plan should communicate, (2) the target audience, and (3) the time period in which the goal should be accomplished. Advertising objectives should be very specific and you must be able to measure the success achieved to know when your goal has been accomplished. Identify the parts of the following objectives.

1. Attract 1,000 new library card holders between the ages of five and ten during January.

   Message: ____

   Target Audience: ____

   Time Period: ____

   Measurement Method: ____

2. Sell 10 percent more floral arrangements to Plainville residents in June.

   Message: ____

   Target Audience: ____

   Time Period: ____

   Measurement Method: ____

3. Increase repeat purchases of store brand goods by 15 percent in the next year.

   Message: ____

   Target Audience: ____

   Time Period: ____

   Measurement Method: ____

4. Sell 120 memberships to individuals referred by existing members in the next six months.

   Message: ____

   Target Audience: ____

   Time Period: ____

   Measurement Method: ____

5. Increase income for the service department by 20 percent next year by encouraging owners of the Convertible Racer to make four maintenance visits each year.

   Message: ____

   Target Audience: ____

   Time Period: ____

   Measurement Method: ____

Activity 2 • Developing the Plan

Directions: Personal computers (PCs) are continually manufactured in smaller and more powerful versions. The newest generation of PCs is a palm-sized version of day planners with computer and memory capabilities. Many companies, including IBM and Apple, have introduced versions of these tiny computers. You work for a competitor of these companies. Your company has developed a handheld PC named *Palm Power*. It has a color screen that is not available on competitors' models, but is priced 15 percent higher. Develop an advertising plan for your company's version of this PC.

Chapter 16

Lesson 16.3 Putting the Ad Plan into Action
LESSON QUIZ

Directions: For each of the following statements, if the statement is true, write a T on the answer line; if the statement is false, write an F on the answer line.

______ 1. The slice-of-life format revolves around people or characters who sing a song or jingle about the product.

______ 2. The technical expertise format involves the manufacturer or producer explaining how the product is made.

______ 3. The scientific evidence format uses characters to represent the product or service, explaining why the service is superior.

______ 4. Timing refers to the schedule on which advertisements will appear in each medium.

______ 5. A recall test asks individuals if they can recognize an advertisement viewed earlier.

______ 6. An advertising agency simply carries out the advertising plan, which is always developed by the organization or business.

______ 7. It is easy to accurately predict the effectiveness of an advertising plan.

Directions: For each of the following items, decide which choice best completes the statement. Write the letter that identifies your choice on the answer line.

______ 8. When selecting an advertising format, one should consider
  A. the music.
  B. the advertising objectives.
  C. technical expertise.
  D. the mood to be portrayed.

______ 9. When advertisers increase their advertising efforts during a specific period of time, this is known as
  A. continuity.
  B. recall.
  C. pulsing.
  D. clutter.

______10. An individual at an advertising agency who works with a business is
  A. part of the business' marketing department.
  B. an account executive.
  C. an employee of the business paying the advertising agency.
  D. all of the above

Activity 1 • Recall Testing

Directions: A large manufacturer of laundry detergent plans to conduct a recall test on an ad that will run in a popular magazine. Two hundred men and women will be given a copy of the magazine and asked to spend as much time as they want reading it. Develop seven questions that the researchers could ask the research participants to determine their level of recognition for the specific advertisement.

1. ____

2. ____

3. ____

4. ____

5. ____

6. ____

7. ____

Activity 2 • Analyzing Print Advertisements

Directions: Choose two advertisements from any print medium and mount them on poster board. Answer the following questions about each ad on separate sheets of paper and attach them to the poster.

1. What is the objective of this ad?
2. Who is the intended target market?
3. What is the theme?
4. What is the format?
5. How would you evaluate the effectiveness of the ad?

Activity 3 • Analyzing Television Advertisements

Directions: Choose one television advertisement. Answer the following questions about the ad.

1. What is the objective of this ad? _______________________________________

2. Who is the intended target market? _____________________________________

3. What is the theme? ____

4. What is the format? ____

5. How would you evaluate the effectiveness of the ad? _____________________

  ©South-Western Publishing Chapter 16

Lesson 17.1 The Value of Selling
LESSON QUIZ

Directions: For each of the following statements, if the statement is true, write a T on the answer line; if the statement is false, write an F on the answer line.

_______ 1. Selling is part of the promotion element of the marketing mix.

_______ 2. Personal selling is meant to communicate with a large group of people.

_______ 3. All promotional methods involve communication with customers.

_______ 4. The information that can be provided in an advertisement is unlimited.

_______ 5. An effective salesperson meets with the customer only once.

_______ 6. Because the company trains its salespeople, the company's managers have complete control over the sales process.

_______ 7. Many salespeople are not paid unless they sell something.

Directions: For each of the following items, decide which choice best completes the statement. Write the letter that identifies your choice on the answer line.

_______ 8. The link between the customer and the business is
  A. advertising.
  B. promotion.
  C. salespeople.
  D. sales.

_______ 9. Customers with similar needs are grouped into
  A. classes.
  B. target markets.
  C. associations.
  D. sales categories.

_______10. Personal selling results in feedback for the
  A. salesperson and the customer.
  B. the business and the salesperson.
  C. the customer and the business.
  D. all of the above

Activity 1 • Selling Starts at the Top

Directions: A recent survey of CEOs in 664 fast-growing companies asked how many hours per week they devoted to sales and marketing based on a 60-hour work week. The following results were gathered.

Company Sales	Hours Per Week	Percentage Per Week
Less than $1 million	23	
$1 million - $5 million	16	
$5 million - $10 million	15	
$10 million - $15 million	15	
$15 million - $20 million	17	
$20 million - $40 million	15	
More than $40 million	17	

1. Complete the column in the chart that identifies the percentage of time spent on sales and marketing each week.
2. What is the average number of hours per week for all companies? _______________________________
3. What is the average percentage of hours for companies under $15 million in sales? _______________
4. Draw a bar graph illustrating the percentage of hours spent on sales and marketing.

5. From this survey, what conclusions can you draw about the importance of sales and marketing to an organization?____

____

____

____

Lesson 17.2 Preparing for Effective Selling
LESSON QUIZ

Directions: For each of the following statements, if the statement is true, write a T on the answer line; if the statement is false, write an F on the answer line.

______ 1. Small distributors gain the advantages of cost-effectiveness and timeliness by using the Internet.

______ 2. Random consumers contacted by salespeople may be upset if they are not interested in the products the salesperson is selling.

______ 3. Company resources are wasted if a contacted consumer is not interested in purchasing a company's products.

______ 4. A marketing-oriented business frequently uses cold calling to find interested consumers.

______ 5. It is not necessary to get a customer's full attention until late in the sales presentation.

______ 6. Every customer experiences a different series of mental stages that lead to a sale.

______ 7. Without assistance from a salesperson, a customer can determine by examining a product if it is the correct one to buy.

Directions: For each of the following items, decide which choice best completes the statement. Write the letter that identifies your choice on the answer line.

______ 8. When a salesperson contacts a large number of people who are conveniently located without knowing a great deal about each person, this is known as
A. sales calls.
B. direct selling.
C. cold calling.
D. market research.

______ 9. A qualified prospective customer should
A. have a need for the product.
B. have the resources to purchase the product.
C. have the authority to make a purchase decision.
D. all of the above

______ 10. Salespeople can gather important information from
A. advertisements.
B. product manuals.
C. trade shows.
D. all of the above

Activity 1 • Selling Is Selling

Directions: Whether you work in a retail store selling shoes or for a large organization selling computer systems, you need to have information. Using the following chart, list information that you would need to complete each sale.

Categories	Shoes	Computers
Customer		
Product		
Competition		

Activity 2 • Information Is Money

Directions: The right information can help a salesperson close a sale. Using the type of information you selected in the previous activity as a guideline, choose a product and research its characteristics and other information that would help you close a sale. Record the information below.

Product: ____

____

____

____

____

____

____

____

____

____

Competition: ____

____

____

____

____

____

____

____

____

____

 ©South-Western Publishing

Name____ Date____________ Class ______________

Lesson 17.3 The Selling Process and Sales Support
LESSON QUIZ

Directions: For each of the following statements, if the statement is true, write a T on the answer line; if the statement is false, write an F on the answer line.

______ 1. During the preapproach, salespeople study target market information.

______ 2. Salespeople often send a letter of introduction or make a telephone call to prospective customers during the preapproach.

______ 3. The sales approach is always made in person.

______ 4. A demonstration should emphasize product features rather than benefits.

______ 5. If a salesperson demonstrates a feature, the customer will recognize the benefit without assistance from the salesperson.

______ 6. Information technology can provide the latest information about products, customers, and competition to help salespeople increase sales.

______ 7. Salespeople rely on distribution, a marketing function, to deliver products to customers when they are needed.

Directions: For each of the following items, decide which choice best completes the statement. Write the letter that identifies your choice on the answer line.

______ 8. When salespeople are paid only by commission, they
   A. will select the target market carefully.
   B. may recommend products and services the customer does not need.
   C. will spend more time preparing a product demonstration.
   D. are motivated only by the desire to help the customer.

______ 9. A salesperson can close the sale by
   A. offering the customer a choice between items.
   B. describing an additional feature of the product.
   C. mentioning that the product has a frequent need for service or repairs.
   D. leaving to assist another customer.

______10. Offering additional supports and services after the initial sale in order to increase customer satisfaction is known as
   A. suggestion selling.
   B. follow-up.
   C. cold calling.
   D. sales support.

Activity 1 • Features and Benefits

Directions: Customers are impressed by benefits rather than features. They want to know what the feature can do for them. For each feature described below, identify the benefit it provides for the customer.

Feature	Benefit
Anti-lock brakes	
Automatic timer on a coffeemaker	
Flat-panel computer monitor	
Stainless steel components	
Adjustable waistband	
Brick exterior	
Prints six pages per minute	
Available in a variety of colors	
Shoulder and hand strap	
Flexible lamp base	

Activity 2 • Job Search

Directions: Every week, businesses advertise for new salespeople. Use your most recent Sunday newspaper or one of the job sites on the Internet. Record the information in the chart below for two advertised sales positions.

Title	Job Description	Amount of Travel	Compensation

©South-Western Publishing

Lesson 18.1 The Expanding World Economy
LESSON QUIZ

Directions: For each of the following statements, if the statement is true, write a T on the answer line; if the statement is false, write an F on the answer line.

______ 1. Most of the products and services produced in the world are still consumed by people in the countries where they are produced.

______ 2. The amount of international trade remains steady from year to year.

______ 3. In the past, manufactured goods made up almost all of the products traded between countries.

______ 4. Today, international trade in services is growing faster than trade in products.

______ 5. One reason for global marketing is the increasing demand for products.

______ 6. Most governments are developing support for businesses that want to increase the amount of business conducted in other countries.

______ 7. Professional and industry associations often provide assistance in international business.

Directions: For each of the following items, decide which choice best completes the statement. Write the letter that identifies your choice on the answer line.

______ 8. Businesses may decide to market products in other countries because
    A. competition is very intense within their domestic market.
    B. companies from other countries entered their own markets.
    C. sales and profits are declining.
    D. all of the above

______ 9. Some business people may choose not to become involved in international trade because
    A. selling products in other countries appears to be complicated.
    B. improvements are being made in transportation methods.
    C. laws prohibit international trade.
    D. all of the above

______ 10. The government provides support for U.S. businesses through
    A. embassies in most countries.
    B. the Small Business Administration.
    C. the U.S. Department of Commerce.
    D. all of the above

Activity 1 • GDP Ranking in 2000

Directions: The gross domestic product (GDP) is the value of all goods and services produced in a country. Ranking countries by their GDP measures and evaluates their production power. Use the library or Internet to find the most recent information to complete the table below.

Country	Rank	GDP
Ecuador		
Malaysia		
Austria		
Peru		
Ireland		
Japan		
Russia		
Egypt		
Hungary		
Zambia		
Sudan		
Norway		
Switzerland		
Singapore		
Israel		
India		
Pakistan		
New Zealand		
Uganda		

Country	Rank	GDP
Guatemala		
Germany		
Belgium		
Morocco		
Bangladesh		
Uganda		
Sweden		
China		
Brazil		
Kenya		
Cuba		
Italy		
Poland		
France		
Argentina		
Canada		
Mexico		
Denmark		
Bolivia		

Activity 2 • Exporting Products

Directions: Select two of the countries identified in the previous activity. Identify the major products and materials the country currently exports.

1. Country:____

   Exports:____

   ____

   ____

2. Country:____

   Exports:____

   ____

   ____

Lesson 18.2 How Businesses Get Involved
LESSON QUIZ

Directions: For each of the following statements, if the statement is true, write a T on the answer line; if the statement is false, write an F on the answer line.

_______ 1. A company involved in indirect exporting takes complete responsibility for marketing its products in other countries.

_______ 2. A negative balance of trade demonstrates that businesses from other countries are satisfying the needs of consumers better than the country's own businesses.

_______ 3. The currency exchange rates fluctuate very little.

_______ 4. Many consumers prefer to purchase products manufactured in their own country.

_______ 5. Currently, a large majority of foreign investments are in manufacturing businesses.

_______ 6. Multinational companies have operations throughout the world and conduct planning for worldwide markets.

_______ 7. Competitors for multinational businesses come from many different locations.

Directions: For each of the following items, decide which choice best completes the statement. Write the letter that identifies your choice on the answer line.

_______ 8. Foreign production has advantages over exporting because
    A. exporting products is difficult.
    B. distribution activities are reduced.
    C. it is easier for investors.
    D. all of the above

_______ 9. A foreign investment occurs when
    A. a consumer purchases a product manufactured in another country.
    B. an investor purchases an existing business in another country.
    C. products are manufactured in another country.
    D. someone in another country purchases an item made in the United States.

_______10. When independent companies develop a relationship to participate in common business activities, this is known as
    A. a foreign investment.
    B. a multinational company.
    C. a joint venture.
    D. normal business operations.

Activity 1 • Exchanging Money

Directions: Every day, companies and individuals all over the world buy and sell goods and services. Sometimes, these exchanges take place between countries and individuals in different countries. Complete the following table with the most recent currency exchange data and use the information to perform the calculations.

	U.S. Dollar	Australia Dollar	United Kingdom Pound	Canada Dollar	Germany Mark	France Franc	Japan Yen	Switzerland Franc	Euro
U.S. Dollar	1								
Australia Dollar		1							
United Kingdom Pound			1						
Canada Dollar				1					
Germany Mark					1				
France Franc						1			
Japan Yen							1		
Switzerland Franc								1	
Euro									1

1. Juniper Inc. in Canada purchased 16 planes from an American company for $115,000 each in U.S. dollars. How much did the company pay in Canadian dollars?

   ____

2. My Maps in Japan purchased 150 maps from a German company for a total of 525 German marks. How much did the company pay in Japanese yen?

   ____

3. Sherman Balloons in the United States purchased a dirigible from an Australian company for 500,000 Australian dollars. How much did the company pay in U.S. dollars?

   ____

4. Faster Flycycles in Australia purchased 1,200 bicycles from a Japanese company for 60 yen each. How much did the company pay in Australian dollars?

   ____

5. A British company purchased 700 video games from a Japanese company for 40 yen each. How much did the company pay in British pounds?

   ____

Lesson 18.3 Understanding International Markets
LESSON QUIZ

Directions: For each of the following statements, if the statement is true, write a T on the answer line; if the statement is false, write an F on the answer line.

______ 1. There are differences in the specific marketing activities that are effective from one country to another.

______ 2. It is not necessary to develop a unique marketing mix to sell products in another country.

______ 3. Preindustrial countries often export manufactured goods.

______ 4. Today, most countries have postindustrial economies.

______ 5. In an industrial economy, the standard of living is higher for most consumers than the standard of living in a postindustrial economy.

______ 6. An increasing standard of living is a sign of a weak economy because few jobs are available and wages are decreasing.

______ 7. Certain words can have very different meanings when translated into another language, making it difficult to use promotions developed in one country in another country.

Directions: For each of the following items, decide which choice best completes the statement. Write the letter that identifies your choice on the answer line.

______ 8. Leaders in preindustrial countries
   A. want more jobs for their citizens.
   B. do not have any interest in moving to another stage.
   C. are satisfied with their country's imports and exports.
   D. all of the above

______ 9. If a country's economy is growing,
   A. there will be more job opportunities.
   B. consumers will have money to spend.
   C. business profits will increase.
   D. all of the above

______ 10. One of the most important factors that can affect the success of international marketing is
   A. the currency exchange rate.
   B. the type of political and legal systems in the country.
   C. the language spoken by the majority of consumers.
   D. all of the above

Activity 1 • Exporting Gum to the United States

Directions: Assume you are a foreign exporter planning to introduce a new brand and flavor of chewing gum to the United States. Using your knowledge of U.S. markets, complete the following chart of marketing functions to describe what you would do to bring your product here.

Marketing Function	Description of Activities
Product/Service Management	
Purchasing	
Selling	
Financing	
Promotion	
Risk Management	
Distribution	
Pricing	
Marketing-Information Management	

Lesson 19.1 Assessing Business Risks
LESSON QUIZ

Directions: For each of the following statements, if the statement is true, write a T on the answer line; if the statement is false, write an F on the answer line.

_______ 1. People invest time and money in new businesses or products when there is a risk of loss because there is also an opportunity for success.

_______ 2. Marketers do not need to understand the risks involved in order to deal with them.

_______ 3. Analyzing risks and opportunities is an important skill for business people only.

_______ 4. A pure risk presents the possibility of an opportunity for great gain.

_______ 5. If your actions do not affect the results of a risk, it is a controllable risk.

_______ 6. Speculative risks are not insurable.

_______ 7. People responsible for risk management go through a careful process to decide the best way to deal with each risk faced by the business.

Directions: For each of the following items, decide which choice best completes the statement. Write the letter that identifies your choice on the answer line.

_______ 8. If a risk is faced by a large number of people, the risk is pure rather than speculative, and the amount of loss can be predicted, it is
A. an insurable risk.
B. a controlled risk.
C. a pure risk.
D. a market risk.

_______ 9. If a business chooses to let another business complete a risky activity for them, they are
A. transferring the risk.
B. avoiding the risk.
C. assuming the risk.
D. insuring the risk.

_______10. A company that assumes a risk
A. purchases insurance to protect the company from the loss.
B. sues the company or individual responsible for any loss.
C. faces the risk and deals with the result.
D. all of the above

Activity 1 • Types of Risk

Directions: For each of the following statements, determine the type of risk in each category.

Event	Type of Risk		
	Pure (P)/ Speculative (S)	**Controllable (C)/ Uncontrollable (U)**	**Insurable (I)/ Uninsurable (U)**
An electrical outage causes the food in your store's freezer to spoil.			
A hailstorm destroys over half of your vegetable crop.			
You install mirrors on the ends of the aisles in your store to detect shoplifters.			
A country to which you export your product places new tariffs on incoming products.			
The FDA releases a report that a chemical you use in your manufacturing process might be considered harmful.			

Activity 2 • Shoplifting and Employee Theft: A Risk Problem

Directions: The owner of a clothing store in a shopping mall estimates that approximately 2 percent of gross sales are lost to shoplifters and employee theft. From your knowledge of risk management and business practices, describe at least three actions the manager might take for each of these problems.

Shoplifting: ____

____

____

____

____

Employee theft: ____

____

____

____

____

 ©South-Western Publishing Chapter 19

Lesson 19.2 Identifying Marketing Risks
LESSON QUIZ

Directions: For each of the following statements, if the statement is true, write a T on the answer line; if the statement is false, write an F on the answer line.

______ 1. Risk management is an important part of the product/service management function.

______ 2. Marketers evaluate opportunities to determine which provide the greatest opportunities with the least risk.

______ 3. New technology and products can enter the market at any time.

______ 4. Some stages of the product life cycle last only a very short time and require the business to make changes to maintain sales and profits.

______ 5. Some elements of the marketing mix are not subject to risks.

______ 6. There are many opportunities for theft as products move through a channel of distribution.

______ 7. One area of risk is the damage that can result from the promotion of other businesses or information communicated by people or other organizations.

Directions: For each of the following items, decide which choice best completes the statement. Write the letter that identifies your choice on the answer line.

______ 8. A major change in operations may be required after
    A. an increase in taxes.
    B. new laws are implemented.
    C. a court ruling goes into effect.
    D. all of the above

______ 9. The product risk that concerns businesses most is
    A. advances incorporated into products produced by other companies.
    B. liability.
    C. spoilage or deterioration if the product is not consumed within a specific time period.
    D. packaging.

______10. Eventually, marketing transactions will become wireless, known as
    A. e-commerce.
    B. w-commerce.
    C. m-commerce.
    D. all of the above

Activity 1 • Risk Management with the Channel of Distribution

Directions: A channel of distribution is the organization and individuals who participate in the movement and exchange of products and services from the producer to the final consumer. Channel members are instrumental in minimizing and often assuming the risk for the manufacturer and retailer. For each of the following questions, determine whether the wholesaler or agent assumes any risk for the products being sold.

Question	Wholesaler of Fresh Vegetables	Wholesaler of Office Supplies	Real Estate Agent
What are the characteristics of the product that will be affected by risk?			
What services or activities must be provided in order to minimize risk?			
Who will be responsible for the distribution?			
Who assumes the risk?			

Activity 2 • Reducing Your Risk

Directions: You are the manager of a large discount store in a large city. Your district manager has given you a checklist of areas where risk management can be improved. List at least two measures you can take to manage risk for each area of concern.

Area of Concern	Risk Management Measures
Customer Safety	
Employee Safety	
Marketing Mix	

　　　©South-Western Publishing　　　Chapter 19

Lesson 19.3 Managing Marketing Risks
LESSON QUIZ

Directions: For each of the following statements, if the statement is true, write a T on the answer line; if the statement is false, write an F on the answer line.

_______ 1. Risk management is so important to the success of a business that it should be incorporated into the company's marketing plan.

_______ 2. A business should always choose business activities that have the least amount of risk.

_______ 3. The strengths and weaknesses of your business should be described in the marketing strategy.

_______ 4. The analysis of market segments to select target markets should include an analysis of the risks that exist in each market.

_______ 5. The action plan in a marketing plan should identify the activities and responsibilities for the marketing strategy.

_______ 6. Most businesses purchase insurance to protect against financial loss.

_______ 7. All marketing personnel should receive special training in safety and security procedures.

Directions: For each of the following items, decide which choice best completes the statement. Write the letter that identifies your choice on the answer line.

_______ 8. A market analysis should identify
   A. marketing strategies.
   B. target markets.
   C. specific activities to reduce risk.
   D. competitors' actions that create risk and opportunity.

_______ 9. A responsibility of the marketing manager is to carefully review each part of the action plan to
   A. verify that all legal requirements are met.
   B. determine if risks are adequately addressed.
   C. assign responsibilities.
   D. proofread the plan for errors.

_______10. Purchasing insurance is a method of
   A. transferring risk.
   B. establishing a marketing strategy.
   C. addressing customer needs.
   D. all of the above

Activity 1 • Risk and the Marketing Functions

Directions: Risk enters into all marketing activities. In order to understand the interrelationships between risk and the marketing functions, list as many areas of risk for each of the following marketing functions as you can.

Marketing Function	Description of Activities
Product/Service Management	
Purchasing	
Selling	
Financing	
Promotion	
Risk Management	
Distribution	
Pricing	
Marketing-Information Management	

Lesson 20.1 Marketing Affects Business Finances
LESSON QUIZ

Directions: For each of the following statements, if the statement is true, write a T on the answer line; if the statement is false, write an F on the answer line.

______ 1. Managing marketing costs is important to the profitability of a business.

______ 2. Finances are not important to non-profit organizations.

______ 3. Marketers are responsible for the revenue and expenses related to marketing activities.

______ 4. When marketers consider changes in the marketing mix, they need to study the costs of the changes and predict the effect on sales.

______ 5. Short-term expenses are for items used within a short time, typically less than five years.

______ 6. Most of the long-term costs to a business are used for marketing.

______ 7. Inventory may be financed through credit extended by the seller.

Directions: For each of the following items, decide which choice best completes the statement. Write the letter that identifies your choice on the answer line.

______ 8. The target market selected by a business determines
    A. the amount of new technology needed by the business.
    B. the amount of sales and revenue that can be obtained.
    C. the responsibilities of the marketer.
    D. all of the above

______ 9. Long-term expenses usually include
    A. advertising and promotion.
    B. salaries and wages.
    C. vehicles and equipment.
    D. all of the above

______10. Supplies are considered to be
    A. a capital expense.
    B. an inventory expense.
    C. an operating expense.
    D. a long-term expense.

Activity 1 • Clipping Revenues and Expenses

Directions: Trina and Pao have been mowing lawns on a part-time basis all through high school. Before next Spring, they are trying to brainstorm a list of new services they can offer. They realize that additional services increase both revenue and expenses. Help Trina and Pao by completing the following table. The first item is completed for you. Fill in the remainder of the table for the items listed.

New Services	Additional Expenses
Seeding and fertilizing	new equipment, material purchase, storage cost of additional materials and equipment, equipment maintenance
Maintaining shrubs	
Offering credit	
Watering grass and plants	

Activity 2 • Categorize Expenses

Directions: Big City Lights is a specialty store offering lighting products and fixtures such as lamps, ceiling lights, garden lights, and other lighting used for homes and offices. The owner plans to open another store in the near future. Complete the following table by identifying possible expenses and assigning them to the appropriate category. The first item is completed for you.

Expense	LongTerm (L) or ShortTerm (S)	Capital (C), Inventory (I), or Operating (O)
Building	L	C

©South-Western Publishing

Lesson 20.2 Tools For Financial Planning
LESSON QUIZ

Directions: For each of the following statements, if the statement is true, write a T on the answer line; if the statement is false, write an F on the answer line.

_______ 1. Financial forecasts are numerical predictions of future performance related to revenue and expenses.

_______ 2. Longer forecasts, developed for a time period such as five years, are usually more accurate than shorter forecasts.

_______ 3. Expense forecasts project changes in the amount the company will need to spend for specific operations or activities.

_______ 4. A single budget is usually developed for all products, markets, and major marketing activities.

_______ 5. The purpose of an income statement is to determine if the business earned a profit or loss on its operations.

_______ 6. An income statement can only be developed for the entire company, not a single operating unit of the company.

_______ 7. Each time a new marketing plan is developed, the marketing manager will identify the most important products and markets for that planning period.

Directions: For each of the following items, decide which choice best completes the statement. Write the letter that identifies your choice on the answer line.

_______ 8. A detailed projection of financial performance for a specific time period, usually a year or less, is a
   A. forecast.
   B. budget.
   C. market share prediction.
   D. sales projection.

_______ 9. The most important financial forecasts for marketing are
   A. sales, market share, and marketing expenses.
   B. sales, marketing expenses, and operating expenses.
   C. budgets, sales, and market share.
   D. short-term expenses, advertising expenses, and distribution expenses.

______10. The most common financial planning method is to
   A. use information from comparable businesses and markets.
   B. look for related figures that help to predict performance.
   C. use past performance.
   D. examine the financial plans of competitors.

Activity 1 • Before and After

Directions: The Save You Money Drug Store planned a major promotional campaign to celebrate its one-year anniversary. Based on information gathered by the management team, an expense forecast was prepared for the promotional campaign. The forecast and actual figures are provided in the following table.

Promotion Expense	Forecast	Actual	Difference
Television	$12,350	$13,500	$______
Radio	3,440	2,990	______
Print	5,000	5,000	______
Coupons	1,500	900	______
Give-aways	6,500	7,350	______
Salaries	4,500	6,500	______
Total	______	______	______

1. Complete the table by calculating the dollar difference between the forecast and actual money spent.
2. The store's annual promotional budget is $150,000. What percentage of the total budget was used for this promotional campaign?

____

3. The annual promotional budget is 10 percent of the store's anticipated yearly net profit. During the two-week anniversary celebration, the store made a net profit of $75,239. What percentage of the anticipated yearly net profit was the profit realized during the promotional sale?

____

Activity 2 • Planning with Marketing Information Systems

Directions: Marketing information management systems play a significant role in capturing and storing information to be used later for financial planning and analysis. For each of the following reports, list several types of information that should be gathered as part of a company's marketing information system.

Sales Forecast:____

____

Market Share:____

____

Customer Accounts:____

____

Income Statement:____

____

Balance Sheet:____

  ©South-Western Publishing Chapter 20

Lesson 20.3 Budgeting For Marketing Activities
LESSON QUIZ

Directions: For each of the following statements, if the statement is true, write a T on the answer line; if the statement is false, write an F on the answer line.

______ 1. The basis for a marketing budget is a marketing strategy.

______ 2. A marketing plan describes the marketing activities to be completed and the resources needed.

______ 3. The marketing mix and budget are not affected by the way the company spent money in the past.

______ 4. Businesses stopped advertising on the Internet because viewers were not responsive to advertising messages.

______ 5. If credit is offered to customers, the sale is not complete.

______ 6. The marketing mix is developed to increase customer satisfaction by offering a product or service that is different from and better than those offered by competitors.

______ 7. The most important source of revenue for the organization is the sale of the secondary products and services that support the primary product.

Directions: For each of the following items, decide which choice best completes the statement. Write the letter that identifies your choice on the answer line.

______ 8. Target markets that the business intends to serve and the marketing mixes to be used for each market are identified by the
A. marketing concept.
B. marketing strategy.
C. advertising plan.
D. media plan.

______ 9. Replacing a product because it is damaged or does not meet the customer's needs
A. reduces the level of sales.
B. reduces customer satisfaction.
C. reduces distribution costs.
D. all of the above

______10. A good indication of where a business is headed is
A. dollar volume of sales.
B. a balance sheet.
C. number of units sold.
D. the current price of the product.

Activity 1 • Financial Skills

Directions: Marketers must be able to develop and use financial statements. Prepare an income statement based on the following information. In addition, calculate the percentage of gross sales for the following: net sales, cost of goods sold, gross margin, total expenses, and net income.

Gross sales, $175,392.36; returns, $1,587.34; beginning inventory, $49,222.43; purchases, $76,234.76; ending inventory, $25,768.45. Expenses for operating the business: salaries, $31,394.22; licenses, $2,547.45; rent, $6,000; advertising, $25,000; professional services, $600; insurance, $1,200; telephone, $1,254.36; postage, $769.33; and utilities, $2,688.67.

INCOME STATEMENT

For period ending ____________

		Percentage of Gross Sales
REVENUE:		
Gross sales		
Returns		
Net sales		%
Beginning inventory		
Purchases		
Cost of goods for sale		
Ending inventory		
Cost of goods sold		%
Gross margin	$	%
EXPENSES:		
Salaries		
Licenses		
Rent		
Advertising		
Professional services		
Insurance		
Telephone		
Postage		
Utilities		
Total expenses	__________	%
NET INCOME	$	%

©South-Western Publishing

Lesson 21.1 What Is Entrepreneurship?
LESSON QUIZ

Directions: For each of the following statements, if the statement is true, write a T on the answer line; if the statement is false, write an F on the answer line.

______ 1. Most investors will read the entire business plan before deciding to make an investment in a specific business.

______ 2. An entrepreneur is an employee and takes direction from the owners of the business.

______ 3. Entrepreneurs only start businesses in the United States.

______ 4. Entrepreneurs cannot start a business based on new marketing ideas.

______ 5. Advertising agencies are involved in the distribution and exchange of products and services between producers and consumers.

______ 6. All small businesses are not owned and operated by entrepreneurs.

______ 7. Small businesses provide about 75% of the all-new jobs.

Directions: For each of the following items, decide which choice best completes the statement. Write the letter that identifies your choice on the answer line.

______ 8. Small businesses make up
   A. almost 25% of all businesses.
   B. about 50% of all businesses.
   C. over 90% of all businesses.
   D. all businesses.

______ 9. Small businesses are responsible for
   A. almost 25% of all goods and services produced.
   B. over 50% of all goods and services produced.
   C. over 90% of all goods and services produced.
   D. all goods and services produced.

______10. Entrepreneurs provided several reasons to become a business owner, including
   A. handling complaints.
   B. earning a large income in the first few years of operation.
   C. providing jobs for community members.
   D. all of the above

Activity 1 • Entrepreneurs Who Succeeded in a Big Way

Directions: Many entrepreneurs have started with a small dream that became a success story that impacted the lives of many investors, employees, and consumers. Well-known entrepreneurs include Henry Ford, Bill Gates, Madame C.J. Walker, Levi Strauss, Ben Cohen, Jerry Greenfield, Margaret Rudkin, Richard Branson, Andrew Carnegie, and Henry Clay Frick, among others. Select one of the listed entrepreneurs. Use the library or Internet to answer the following questions.

Date of birth: _______________________________   Date of death: _______________________

Brief personal history: ____

____

____

____

____

Description of business environment: ____

____

____

____

Business history: ____

____

____

____

Major industry impacted: ____

Changes to the industry: ____

____

____

____

____

Impact on consumers: ____

____

____

____

____

Impact on history: ____

____

____

____

____

          ©South-Western Publishing   Chapter 21

Lesson 21.2 Entrepreneurs' Characteristics
LESSON QUIZ

Directions: For each of the following statements, if the statement is true, write a T on the answer line; if the statement is false, write an F on the answer line.

______ 1. An individual can develop the necessary skills to become an entrepreneur.

______ 2. Entrepreneurs enjoy team activities and cooperate well with others.

______ 3. You can be a small business owner without being an entrepreneur.

______ 4. Business experience is an important part of preparing to become a successful entrepreneur.

______ 5. Most of the people who start successful businesses today have completed high school and often have one or more college degrees.

______ 6. Entrepreneurs often work for another company for many years before starting their own businesses.

______ 7. Many entrepreneurs suffered one or more business failures before they became skilled business people.

Directions: For each of the following items, decide which choice best completes the statement. Write the letter that identifies your choice on the answer line.

______ 8. To become a successful entrepreneur, your academic preparation should include
    A. technological skills.
    B. communication skills.
    C. math skills.
    D. all of the above

______ 9. Some companies now ask employees to sign legal agreements that they will not
    A. develop an idea for the business.
    B. start a business from an idea developed on the job.
    C. accept profits from the company generated by an idea develop by the employee.
    D. all of the above

______ 10. Scientific skills important to entrepreneurs include
    A. statistics.
    B. public speaking.
    C. problem identification.
    D. all of the above

Activity 1 • Preparing to Be an Entrepreneur

Directions: Every entrepreneur is a unique individual, even though they may share common characteristics. Rate yourself on a scale of 1 to 10 for the entrepreneurial characteristics listed below and explain the rating.

Focused and goal oriented:

1   2   3   4   5   6   7   8   9   10

Explanation: ____

____

____

Risk taking:

Explanation: ____

____

____

Desire to achieve:

1   2   3   4   5   6   7   8   9   10

Explanation: ____

____

____

Independence:

1   2   3   4   5   6   7   8   9   10

Explanation: ____

Self-confidence:

1   2   3   4   5   6   7   8   9   10

Explanation: ____

____

____

Creativity:

1   2   3   4   5   6   7   8   9   10

Explanation: ____

____

____

          ©South-Western Publishing

Lesson 21.3 Business Ownership Opportunities
LESSON QUIZ

Directions: For each of the following statements, if the statement is true, write a T on the answer line; if the statement is false, write an F on the answer line.

_______ 1. Specialized areas such as farming and fitness training provide entrepreneurship opportunities.

_______ 2. Nearly 50 percent of small businesses use the Internet as a regular part of their business.

_______ 3. Research studies summarized by the Small Business Administration report that half of all small businesses use the Internet for business transactions, either to sell or buy products.

_______ 4. An auction house is a business related to the pricing function.

_______ 5. It is important for an entrepreneur to choose a business that he or she likes and has the interests and skills to operate successfully.

_______ 6. Many entrepreneurial businesses gather information, prepare reports for businesses, or provide data security services for other companies.

_______ 7. Most new businesses will offer significant competition to any existing businesses.

Directions: For each of the following items, decide which choice best completes the statement. Write the letter that identifies your choice on the answer line.

_______ 8. Retailers and wholesalers are marketing businesses because they
    A. earn a profit.
    B. accumulated products from manufacturers and make them available to consumers.
    C. operate in every state.
    D. all of the above

_______ 9. Business opportunities related to selling include
    A. express delivery businesses.
    B. advertising agencies.
    C. businesses that offer sales training.
    D. all of the above

_______10. An entrepreneur should begin with
    A. an idea for a product or service.
    B. studying the market.
    C. developing a business.
    D. developing a marketing mix to meet the needs of the customers.

Activity 1 • Business Ideas

Directions: Many skills can be turned into a unique business. Complete the following table. Describe a unique business that can be created from the skill identified on the left.

Skill	Unique Business
Painting	
Researching	
Physical Fitness	
Computer Programming	
Negotiating	
Teaching	

Activity 2 • Opportunities for Competition

Directions: Select a business that you visit frequently. Pretend that you plan to establish a business that will compete with the existing business. Answer the following questions.

Strengths of the existing business: ____

____

____

Weaknesses of the existing business: ____

____

____

Why your business will compete successfully: ____

____

____

Lesson 21.4 Legal Needs for Entrepreneurs
LESSON QUIZ

Directions: For each of the following statements, if the statement is true, write a T on the answer line; if the statement is false, write an F on the answer line.

______ 1. The corporation is the most common form of business ownership, with over three-quarters of all businesses organized in this way.

______ 2. Corporations are owned by people who purchase stock in the company.

______ 3. Under the proprietorship form of organization, the owner is responsible for the money needed to start and operate the business as well as all business planning and management.

______ 4. Partnerships pool the knowledge and skills of all the owners and employees.

______ 5. Banks are more likely to loan money to proprietorships than partnerships.

______ 6. Because a corporation has many owners, it faces fewer rules and regulations than other forms of business.

______ 7. A partnership is formed using a charter.

Directions: For each of the following items, decide which choice best completes the statement. Write the letter that identifies your choice on the answer line.

______ 8. Advantages of a corporation include
    A. if money is owed, each owner is liable for the debt.
    B. owners are liable for the decisions and actions of the corporation.
    C. the business continues to operate even if one owner decides to sell his or her stock.
    D. all of the above

______ 9. Corporations are usually taxed
    A. at a higher rate than other forms of business.
    B. at a lower rate than other forms of business.
    C. at the same rate as other forms of business.
    D. at a rate that various from year to year.

______10. Legal steps for starting a business include
    A. register the name of your new business.
    B. prepare to collect and report taxes.
    C. obtain financing for purchases and business operations.
    D. all of the above

Activity 1 • Business Name

Directions: The name of a business creates an image for potential customers. Complete the following table. Create a name for each business described below. Check sources such as the phone book and Internet to verify that the name is unique.

Description	Name	Unique (Yes or No)
Dog obedience training school		
Architect who designs single-family residences		
Creates ice sculptures for weddings, conferences, and other events		
Store that sells and repairs bicycles		
Design and manufacture camping equipment		
Tutor high school students in various academic subjects		

Activity 2 • Public Corporations

Directions: Shares of many companies are publicly traded on a stock exchange. These companies are listed in the newspaper and on the Internet, among other locations. Select one of the publicly traded companies and answer the following questions.

Name of company: _______________________   Stock symbol: _______________________

Current stock price: _______________________   Stock exchange: _______________________

Product or service: ____

Location of company: ____

Web site for company: ____

Investment potential: ____

Explanation of investment rating: ____

Lesson 21.5 Developing a Business Plan
LESSON QUIZ

Directions: For each of the following statements, if the statement is true, write a T on the answer line; if the statement is false, write an F on the answer line.

______ 1. The characteristics of entrepreneurs make them more interested in operating the business than developing plans for a business.

______ 2. Entrepreneurs should have help available when problems are encountered and decisions must be made.

______ 3. A business plan guides the development and operation of a new business.

______ 4. A business plan is not necessary if it is used only by the entrepreneur.

______ 5. A business plan is never used by the employees of a business.

______ 6. Bankers and investors need only a general overview of the business to determine if it is a solid financial investment.

______ 7. Lawyers, accountants, and advertising agencies may read a business plan to determine if a business is prepared to work with them.

Directions: For each of the following items, decide which choice best completes the statement. Write the letter that identifies your choice on the answer line.

______ 8. Every business plan should contain
  A. a description of the individuals reading the plan.
  B. a description of the type of competition the business will face.
  C. a description of each employee the business will need.
  D. all of the above

______ 9. A business plan will help an entrepreneur
  A. make decisions about the business.
  B. determine the personal characteristics needed for success.
  C. accumulate more savings for establishing the business.
  D. sell additional products.

______10. The summary in a business plan should
  A. provide details about the products and services sold by the business.
  B. provide an overview of the business.
  C. describe the specific needs and purchase behavior of the target market.
  D. describe the organization of the departments in the business.

Activity 1 • Information for a Business Plan

Directions: Pretend that you plan to establish a business. You will need to gather information and make decisions to create a business plan. Choose a business you would like to establish and answer the following questions.

Name of business: ____

Description of products and services: _______________________________

____

Names of owners: ____

Form of ownership: ____

Main business objective: ____

Major strength: ____

Major weakness: ____

Current economic environment: _____________________________________

Main competitor: ____

Description of target market: _______________________________________

____

Needs of the target market: ____

Sales forecast: ____

Major departments in organization: __________________________________

Equipment and resources needed: ___________________________________

____

Staffing requirements: ____

____

Description of marketing mix: _______________________________________

____

____

____

Resources needed for marketing: ____________________________________

____

____

 ©South-Western Publishing

Lesson 22.1 Managing with a Purpose
LESSON QUIZ

Directions: For each of the following statements, if the statement is true, write a T on the answer line; if the statement is false, write an F on the answer line.

______ 1. Effective managers are able to organize the resources and work of a company in ways that result in success.

______ 2. Necessary resources must be available or a task cannot be performed.

______ 3. Effective marketing requires few people and a limited amount of resources.

______ 4. The work of only your company needs to be coordinated as products move through a channel of distribution.

______ 5. Long-range planning is easy because it relies on information from a variety of sources.

______ 6. Long-range planning is often known as operational planning.

______ 7. Some functions are common to all managers, no matter where they work or their level in the organization.

Directions: For each of the following items, decide which choice best completes the statement. Write the letter that identifies your choice on the answer line.

______ 8. Standards were announced for seven new Internet ad formats because
    A. ads were taking up too much space on web pages.
    B. advertisements did not fit easily on a web page.
    C. the success rate of existing standards was low.
    D. all of the above

______ 9. Marketing managers are responsible for
    A. identifying markets and planning marketing mixes.
    B. manufacturing the product.
    C. hiring all employees.
    D. all of the above

______ 10. The activities needed to match individuals with the work to be done are known as
    A. organizing.
    B. staffing.
    C. leading.
    D. controlling.

Activity 1 • Dividing Time

Directions: Interview a manager of a local business and determine how much of the manager's time is spent on each of the five management functions. Prepare a pie chart in the space below that illustrates the percentage of an average work week spent on each function. Bring your findings to class and share them with your classmates. How are they the same or different? Combine your results with other class members to determine averages. Are there any conclusions you can draw from your findings and those of your classmates?

Activity 2 • Lists of Five

Directions: For each of the following management functions, list five activities that a marketing manager might perform.

Planning: ____

____

____

Organizing:____

____

____

Controlling: ____

____

____

Staffing: ____

____

____

Leading: ____

____

____

Lesson 22.2 Managing Effectively with a Plan
LESSON QUIZ

Directions: For each of the following statements, if the statement is true, write a T on the answer line; if the statement is false, write an F on the answer line.

______ 1. Most successful companies develop written business plans.

______ 2. Most companies require each manager to prepare written operational plans to show how their plans support the marketing plan.

______ 3. In the market analysis portion of a marketing plan, managers learn about specific activities they need to perform.

______ 4. The marketing strategy section of a marketing plan describes the competition and the economy.

______ 5. Much of the organizing work in a company should be done after a marketing plan is developed.

______ 6. The responsibilities of most managers will not change, regardless of the number of marketing plans produced.

______ 7. Poor performance only occurs when people do not have the skills to do the work.

Directions: For each of the following items, decide which choice best completes the statement. Write the letter that identifies your choice on the answer line.

______ 8. A company will not want to change its basic organizational structure unless
   A. it sees ways to improve performance.
   B. a manager leaves the company.
   C. all managers agree to the organizational change.
   D. all of the above

______ 9. A Japanese corporate tradition that stifles any questioning of management decisions is
   A. the practice of paying cash rather than checks to employees.
   B. promotion based on seniority.
   C. pressure from foreign corporations.
   D. the size of most Japanese corporations.

______10. An environmental factor that causes businesses to change their plans is
   A. new technology.
   B. competition.
   C. laws and regulations.
   D. all of the above

Activity 1 • Advertising Your Management Policies

Directions: Often companies use their management policies or philosophies as headlines or taglines for their promotional campaigns. An example of this is Ford Motor Company using "Quality is Job 1" as a theme. Look through current magazines and newspapers and identify three advertisements that use a management philosophy in their promotional copy. Cut out these advertisements and paste them on a piece of paper. Answer the following questions.

1. Which management philosophy or policy is being emphasized?
2. What does the company want to accomplish by using this philosophy or policy in the company's advertising?

Activity 2 • Company Goals and Outcomes

Directions: Planning and controlling are interrelated management functions. Usually, a company goal includes a specific outcome or objective so the goal can be measured and evaluated. For the following general business problems, write a company goal that includes a specific measurable outcome. The first objective is completed as an example.

1. The Eastside store needs an increase in sales volume. _______________________________

2. Supply costs have increased 10 percent. _______________________________

3. Employee accidents are most frequent on Fridays. _______________________________

4. Customer surveys indicate customers would like the store to stay open later in the evenings. _______________________________

5. Employee morale seems to be low. _______________________________

6. Employees are leaving the company for higher salaries at other businesses. _______________________________

Lesson 22.3 Managing Marketing Activities
LESSON QUIZ

Directions: For each of the following statements, if the statement is true, write a T on the answer line; if the statement is false, write an F on the answer line.

_______ 1. The activities managers perform while carrying out business management functions vary.

_______ 2. A manager may choose to implement monthly and weekly plans.

_______ 3. Company policies and procedures determine the organization structure for marketing.

_______ 4. Managers are not responsible for filling staff openings with the most qualified people.

_______ 5. Managers are never responsible for marketing and selling products directly to customers.

_______ 6. Most sales managers do not actively train new salespeople or improve the selling skills of experienced employees.

_______ 7. Leadership skills are important only for senior managers.

Directions: For each of the following items, decide which choice best completes the statement. Write the letter that identifies your choice on the answer line.

_______ 8. Marketing activities can be organized by
  A. geography.
  B. market.
  C. product.
  D. all of the above

_______ 9. The legality of an employer's actions in monitoring employee activity is not usually questioned because
  A. a business must earn a profit.
  B. new technology enables managers to monitor activity more closely.
  C. employee activities are conducted on company time using company property.
  D. all of the above

______10. The major controlling activity of managers is to
  A. gather and review information to determine if objectives, plans, and standards are met.
  B. develop the standards for performance of the company's marketing activities.
  C. correct mistakes that cause marketing problems.
  D. revise the marketing plan.

Activity 1 • Determining Staffing Needs

Directions: Use the information provided to answer the following questions and develop a work schedule.

Sarah Mendez is opening a boutique. The operating hours of the store will be Monday through Friday: 10:00 a.m. until 8:00 p.m.; Saturday: 10:00 a.m. until 5:00 p.m. Sarah needs one full-time person for each of the days, 10:00 until 5:00. She also needs two part-time workers at night from 4:00 until 9:00. On Saturday, she wants two staff people to work from opening until one hour past closing. She has interviewed many applicants and has decided to hire the following people.

José—can work after 3:00 p.m. on Mondays, Wednesdays, and Fridays.
Tara—can work 10:00 until 5:00 every day except Thursdays.
Jim—can work every Saturday and Tuesday night.
Linda—can work every other Saturday and all day Thursdays and Mondays.
Fred—can work every evening.
Ann—can work every other Saturday and one or two days during the week.

1. Complete the following work schedule for the boutique by identifying the days and times each employee will work.

	Mon.	Tues.	Wed.	Thurs.	Fri.	Sat.
10:00						
11:00						
12:00						
1:00						
2:00						
3:00						
4:00						
5:00						
6:00						
7:00						
8:00						
9:00						

2. Are all work days covered with the necessary number of employees?

3. If not, what else does Sarah need?

4. If Sarah pays $5.25 per hour to her employees, what will be her weekly salary costs based on the number of hours currently covered?

 ©South-Western Publishing

Chapter 22

Lesson 23.1 Benefits of a Marketing Career
LESSON QUIZ

Directions: For each of the following statements, if the statement is true, write a T on the answer line; if the statement is false, write an F on the answer line.

______ 1. People who are not directly employed in marketing jobs do not need to use marketing skills as part of their work.

______ 2. Owners of small businesses need to perform marketing activities to make their businesses successful.

______ 3. Marketing people are involved in many of our daily activities.

______ 4. Businesses that provide products and services to other businesses do not need marketing personnel.

______ 5. International marketing is providing fewer career opportunities each year.

______ 6. As companies develop new products and services for identifying new market opportunities, marketers are involved from the beginning.

______ 7. When economic conditions are poor, marketing employees are often the first to be reduced and the last to be rehired.

Directions: For each of the following items, decide which choice best completes the statement. Write the letter that identifies your choice on the answer line.

______ 8. In the United States, marketing jobs are
   A. about 15 percent of all jobs.
   B. 25–33 percent of all jobs.
   C. about 50 percent of all jobs.
   D. about 75 percent of all jobs.

______ 9. A study by the U.S. Department of Labor determined that the most important competency employees need to perform their jobs is
   A. math skills.
   B. scientific skills.
   C. communications skills.
   D. physical skills.

______10. The most common reason why a person is not considered when a position is filled in an organization is
   A. lack of appropriate preparation.
   B. unreasonable compensation requests by the potential employee.
   C. geographic limitations.
   D. disability.

Activity 1 • Getting Ready

Directions: Picture the professional position you would like to have ten years from now. Use the library or Internet to discover more information about the position and the preparations you need to complete to hold the position. Answer the following questions.

Job title: ____

Salary: ____

Responsibilities: ____

____

____

Academic requirements: ___________________________________

____

____

Companies that have this position: ___________________________

____

____

Activity 2 • Help Wanted

Directions: Examine the classified advertisements in your local newspaper. Select an available marketing position. Use the advertisement, library, or Internet to gather information about the position and the company.

Job title: ____

Salary: ____

Responsibilities: ____

____

____

Marketing tasks: ____

____

____

Skills needed: ____

____

____

Name of company: _______________________________________

Location of company: _____________________________________

Company's primary product or service: ________________________

Size of company: ____

Lesson 23.2 Job Levels in Marketing
LESSON QUIZ

Directions: For each of the following statements, if the statement is true, write a T on the answer line; if the statement is false, write an F on the answer line.

______ 1. Career planning increases your chances for a successful career.

______ 2. The knowledge and skills needed to be successful in a job will not change over time.

______ 3. Upper-level marketing positions require only a high school diploma.

______ 4. People who perform career planning are more likely to have jobs they like.

______ 5. Most people who hold entry-level positions do not view the job as the first step in a career path.

______ 6. A marketing specialist usually has a four-year college degree.

______ 7. Traditional marketing jobs are disappearing because of the growth of the Internet.

Directions: For each of the following items, decide which choice best completes the statement. Write the letter that identifies your choice on the answer line.

______ 8. The levels of employment in marketing, in the correct sequence, are
   A. entry, specialist, career, supervisor/manager, and executive/entrepreneur.
   B. entry, supervisor/manager, career, specialist, and executive/entrepreneur.
   C. specialist, career, entry, executive/entrepreneur, and supervisor/manager.
   D. entry, career, specialist, supervisor/manager, and executive/entrepreneur.

______ 9. A manager
   A. has the greatest amount of authority and responsibility for marketing.
   B. must have effective communications, human relations, and leadership skills.
   C. often has a graduate degree in business.
   D. all of the above

______10. Interpersonal skills are important to marketers because they
   A. work with people on their marketing team.
   B. communicate with customers to solve problems.
   C. are involved regularly with people inside and outside of the company.
   D. all of the above

Activity 1 • Marketing Communication

Directions: Marketing communication doesn't always directly sell a product. It is also involved in solving problems. Describe how you would handle the following customers' complaints.

Roberta Flagg purchased a washer and dryer from your store. Repairmen have made two visits to her home to make repairs. She is still dissatisfied with the performance of the appliances.

____

____

____

____

Jeffrey Smith has complained that a sales representative was rude when he asked for assistance.

____

____

____

____

Grace Wilson recently purchased a dining room table. When it was delivered, a long scratch was made in her dining room wall and a mirror was broken.

____

____

____

____

Activity 2 • Internal Marketing Communication

Directions: Marketing communication also occurs within a business. Describe how you would handle the following situations.

After working as a salesclerk for a year, you would like to request an increase in salary.

____

____

____

____

Your supervisor is not happy with your work. You have been late twice this week and you have not completed the tasks assigned to you.

____

____

____

Lesson 23.3 Marketing Education and Career Paths
LESSON QUIZ

Directions: For each of the following statements, if the statement is true, write a T on the answer line; if the statement is false, write an F on the answer line.

______ 1. Many high schools offer business and marketing classes as electives designed to develop general knowledge of marketing principles.

______ 2. A Marketing Education program provides information for high school students considering full-time employment in marketing after graduation.

______ 3. Community colleges enable students to earn a Bachelor's degree.

______ 4. Cooperative education provides work experience.

______ 5. All employees would choose to move into a management position if given the opportunity.

______ 6. In recent years, businesses have reduced the number of levels of management and given the employees more responsibility and authority.

______ 7. You can choose a career path based on industry, marketing function, or geographic location.

Directions: For each of the following items, decide which choice best completes the statement. Write the letter that identifies your choice on the answer line.

______ 8. An Associate of Arts degree
  A. is a one-year diploma program.
  B. is a step toward a Bachelor's degree.
  C. prepares graduates for specialist-level positions.
  D. all of the above

______ 9. Marketers can continue to educate themselves after employment by
  A. earning a Master of Business Administration.
  B. attending conferences and seminars.
  C. reading business and marketing magazines.
  D. all of the above

______10. More than a quarter of all overseas work assignments end early because
  A. the employee's task is complete.
  B. the employee or family members cannot adjust to the assignment.
  C. the employee does not know the language.
  D. enough entertainment is not provided.

Activity 1 • Career Path

Directions: Match the employment positions on the left with the career paths on the right. Place the employment positions in the correct sequence in each career path.

Positions	Nursing	Firefighting
Project Leader Licensed Practical Nurse District Leader Station Chief Nurse Practitioner Assistant Manager Consultant Regional Director of Operations Fire Inspector Manager Fire Chief Senior Associate Registered Nurse Store Manager Vice President	Nurse's Aide ↓ ↓ ↓	Firefighter ↓ ↓ ↓
	Sales	**Technology**
	Customer Service Rep ↓ ↓ ↓ ↓	Associate ↓ ↓ ↓ ↓ ↓

Activity 2 • Career Possibilities

Directions: For each area of interest, provide five possible jobs that use the skill. Try to think of jobs in a variety of career fields and industries. The first one has been completed for you.

Skill	Jobs
Writing	technical writer, editor, speech writer, novelist, journalist
Photography	
History	
Sports	
Cooking	
Golf	

　　　©South-Western Publishing　　　

Lesson 23.4 Beginning Career Planning
LESSON QUIZ

Directions: For each of the following statements, if the statement is true, write a T on the answer line; if the statement is false, write an F on the answer line.

______ 1. People often move into totally different areas of work than they originally planned.

______ 2. Employers value experience because it demonstrates your motivation.

______ 3. It is not easy to find an entry-level job in marketing.

______ 4. Planning is an important marketing skill.

______ 5. Many companies use their web sites to post available jobs.

______ 6. Performance reviews from previous employers should not be incorporated into your career portfolio.

______ 7. A career portfolio will help you complete a job application.

Directions: For each of the following items, decide which choice best completes the statement. Write the letter that identifies your choice on the answer line.

______ 8. In the year 2,000, most employees worked in the
    A. manufacturing field.
    B. service field.
    C. retail field.
    D. wholesale field.

______ 9. You can add to work experience by
    A. completing an internship.
    B. volunteering in community organizations.
    C. participating in school activities.
    D. all of the above

______10. A career portfolio
    A. demonstrates your experience.
    B. contains information about jobs for which you have applied.
    C. identifies potential employers.
    D. all of the above

Activity 1 • Application Worksheet

Directions: The following questions can be used to help you prepare a resume or complete an application.

Name: ____

Address: ____

____

Job objective: ____

____

Education: ____

____

____

Skills: ____

____

____

____

Work experience: ____

____

____

____

Activities: ____

____

____

____

Interests: ____

____

____

____

Skills: ____

____

____

____

Accomplishments: ____

____

____

